HIPAA PRIVACY OFFICER

DAVE SWEIGERT

M.Sci., CISA, CISSP, HCISPP, PMP, Security+

DEDICATION

This book is dedicated -- firstly -- to the brave men and women that have answered the call to serve in a trauma medicine related role. This includes: trauma surgeons, emergency room nurses, flight nurses; but, especially paramedics and emergency medical technicians (EMTs) of the pre-hospital service.

Every day hundreds of Americans are cared for by the skillful personnel that fill these ranks. This dedication also recognizes the selfless individuals that staff emergency 911 dispatch centers, professionals that literally "answer the call".

This essay is also dedicated to the professional men and women working in the trade of protecting medical information and protecting the sacred right of patient privacy. This includes Privacy Officers, Information Security Officers and Facility Security Officers.

Thank you all for your service.

Contents

Dave Sweigert

PREFACE

This short booklet was created in response to the ANTHEM data breach of February 2015 and the myriad of news stories in the medical and health industry creating angst and anxiety over impending data breach fines and sanctions.

Most of these articles purport to "warn" readers that in this post-ANTHEM world federal auditors will soon begin a HIPAA witch hunt and that organizations caught unaware will pay hundreds of thousands of dollars in fines to the government.

The objective of this booklet is to provide the HIPAA novice with a simple blueprint to begin building an audit readiness program to prepare for a possible incident requiring the demonstration of compliance activities; such as a data breach investigation or "HIPAA compliance audit".

This guide is for the well-meaning mid-sized organization that wants to do the right thing, but, doesn't know where to start.

The reader will accomplish two learning outcomes:
(1) gain a basic understanding of audit principles and concepts, and (2) build the foundations for a realistic HIPAA compliance program.

Unfortunately, the subject of HIPAA compliance is viewed as a dry and boring subject. Therefore, the author has taken license to over-simplify some of the more complex concepts and inject a sufficient amount of humor to ease the burden of learning regulatory compliance concepts.

DISCLAIMER: The author advises the reader that any serious HIPAA compliance program cannot be created with an overnight fix. A wise reader will consult with legal advisors and attorneys about the more complex concepts that could bring legal liability upon an organization. In this context, this booklet is a layman's practitioner guide, not a legal opinion. The author is a non-attorney who is not providing legal advice.

IMAGES: The majority of the images in this work have been procured from federal, state or local government web-sites. In some cases, images that have been identified as common work and public domain have been used.

Public Law 104–191
104th Congress

An Act

To amend the Internal Revenue Code of 1986 to improve portability and continuity of health insurance coverage in the group and individual markets, to combat waste, fraud, and abuse in health insurance and health care delivery, to promote the use of medical savings accounts, to improve access to long-term care services and coverage, to simplify the administration of health insurance, and for other purposes.

Be it enacted by the Senate and House of Representatives of the United States of America in Congress assembled,

SECTION 1. SHORT TITLE; TABLE OF CONTENTS.

(a) SHORT TITLE.—This Act may be cited as the "Health Insurance Portability and Accountability Act of 1996".

(b) TABLE OF CONTENTS.—The table of contents of this Act is as follows:

Federal HIPAA law

INTRODUCTION

In February 2015 ANTHEM Blue Cross, Blue Shield (Indianapolis, Indiana) made a public announcement that nearly 80 million records of personally identifiable informatin had been "hacked". This seminal event has raised the awareness of the American public as to the protection of patient privacy.

Within less than a week, several mass tort lawsuits had been filed against ANTHEM. Several state Attorneys General have initiated investigations against ANTHEM. These lawsuits and investigations will instruct the legal community, especially plaintiff's lawyers, about another mass tort cause of action -- the data breach tort lawsuit. With such awareness, it is predicated that the amount of potential class action tort lawsuits against organizations involved in a data breach of medical information will soon skyrocket.

Whether preparing for an audit, or defending oneself in a court of law, the principles and concepts contained in this booklet will be invaluable in building a strong defense for the organization.

This booklet is designed to give the novice HIPAA pratitioner an immediate jump start to launch some of the most practical activities to achieve "quick wins" that will demonstrate to the organization their personal competency in developing a successful HIPAA compliance program.

The following chapters will help the layman prepare to step into the shoes of a HIPAA audit practitioner that has been tasked to demonstrate compliance with HIPAA/HITECH.

The end-goal will always be protecting patient privacy.

BASICS

I. LEGAL FRAMEWORK

DISCLAIMER: At the outset, the reader is advised that the author is a non-attorney who is not providing legal advice.

A few examples of recent headlines that describe well-meaning organizations that have been "burned by HIPAA".

- PARKVIEW HOSPITAL FINED **$800,000** FOR HIPAA VIOLATIONS

- ALASKA DEPARTMENT OF HEALTH AND HUMAN SERVICES (DHHS) FINED **$1,7000,000**

- NEW YORK PRESBYTERIAN HOSPITAL FINED **$4.8 MILLION** FOR HIPAA BREACH

The federal government has shown no signs of easing off aggressive investigations and auditing of institutions struggling with protecting sensitive medical data. In fact, the government has announced sweeping auditing programs to shortly begin (2015) that will undoubtedly bring more headlines.

The reader may correctly surmise that such massive fines were the result of breaches of medical information; commonly known as a **data breach** to the layman. True. But, the investigation into what caused the data breach will delve into the organizational practices and possible negligence that led up to the data breach incident.

The more disjointed and unorganized the data protection activities appear to be, the more likely fines and sanctions will be increased as a warning to other organizations. Additionally, besides federal investigations, such data breaches result in litigation activity and the possibility of millions of dollars in damages[1].

Before continuing further, the reader should decide if they want to efficiently and gracefully build an effective data governance and compliance program that will protect the sensitive medical information entrusted to their organization, governance that will demonstrate good faith compliance to outside auditors and investigators and reduce overall risk and liability to the organization.

That is the focus of this booklet, to help those serious minded individuals quickly align resources and organizational processes to protect sensitive data and reduce the risk of being "HIPAA road kill" and the next industry headline.

The alternative is to muddle through with the same old ineffective half measures that will make it clear to a jury, administrative law judge, news reporter or patient that other corporate priorities were more important to senior management; like employee parties, dress-up days, hot dog socials and baby picture guessing contests.

The end game: demonstrate that organizational priorities put protecting the sacred right of patient privacy at the top of this list.

MORE ORGANIZATIONS CAUGHT UNAWARE

It is anticipated by the industry press that many organizations will soon be caught off guard by investigations and audits conducted under the authority of the Health Insurance Portability and Accountability Act (HIPAA) of 1996[2].

---

[1] *Curry v. AvMed, Inc.*, No. 11-13694, 2012 WL 2012 WL 3833035, — F.3d —- (11th Cir. Sep. 5, 2012).

[2] (HIPAA) (Pub L 104–191, 110 Stat 1936).

These organizations will be surprised to discover that they are indeed an entity that can be investigated by the U.S. Department of Health and Human Services (HHS).

Recent changes in federal laws and implementing regulations of the federal HIPAA law have expanded the scope of the regulatory reach of HHS.

Examples of services provided by organizations that might believe they are not a regulated entity under the federal HIPAA law include:

- counseling, service, assessment, or procedure regarding a physical or mental condition; and,
- preventive, diagnostic, rehabilitative, maintenance, or palliative care; and,
- sale or dispensing of a drug, device, equipment, or other item in accordance with a prescription, and,
- accounting, book-keeping, bill collecting, legal services firm; and,
- Internet-based Cloud Services Providers (CSP) offering off-site storage of bulk data, etc., etc.

Prior to 2013, for the most part HIPAA only touched "covered entities"[3] (CE), such as community hospitals, the offices of physicians, health plans, health payment clearinghouses, etc.

---

[3] A covered entity is a health plan, a health care clearinghouse, or a health care provider that conducts any standard electronic transactions. The standard electronic transactions are those provided in the Transactions and Code Sets Rule such as enrollment or claims payment.

[45 C.F.R. § 160.103 (definition of covered entity)]

Many of these so-called CEs have been aware of the implications of HIPAA for many years and have mature compliance programs. However, these CEs have been contracting for outsourced services to **business associates** who haven't been held to the same privacy and data security standards – until now[4].

Several recent federal laws have expanded the privacy protections required by HIPAA to contractors and business associates that work with CEs.

----

[4] Examples of Business Associates

- A third party administrator that assists a health plan with claims processing.
- A CPA firm whose accounting services to a health care provider involve access to protected health information.
- An attorney whose legal services to a health plan involve access to protected health information.
- A consultant that performs utilization reviews for a hospital.
- A health care clearinghouse that translates a claim from a non-standard format into a standard transaction on behalf of a health care provider and forwards the processed transaction to a payer.
- An independent medical transcriptionist that provides transcription services to a physician.
- A pharmacy benefits manager that manages a health plan's pharmacist network.

http://www.hhs.gov/ocr/privacy/hipaa/understanding/coveredentities/businessassociates.html

The Health Information Technology for Economic and Clinical Health Act ("the HITECH Act")[5], amplified patient privacy protections in the HIPAA Privacy Rule, Security Rule, Enforcement Rule and Breach Notification Rule and expanded regulatory reach to organizations previously exempted.

The graphic below will help the reader understand the current regulatory rule framework.

PRIVACY RULE	SECURITY RULE	ENFORCEMENT RULE	BREACH NOTIFICATION RULE

BUSINESS ASSOCIATES MANDATORY COMPLIANCE

Under the new regulatory umbrella, modified by HIPAA, HIPAA now reaches the **"business associate"** (**BA**). BAs are those ancillary entities that provide services and support to CEs. Certain aspects of the Privacy Rule and the entirety of the Security Rule are now applied to BAs by what is known as the HIPAA Omnibus Rule[6].

For example, BAs have been required to demonstrate compliance with parts of HIPAA's Privacy Rule and the entirety of Security Rule since the compliance deadline of **September 23, 2013**.

---

[5] Part of the American Recovery and Reinvestment Act of 2009 (ARRA) (Pub L 111-5, 123 Stat 115), the HITECH Act significantly modifies the Health Insurance Portability and Accountability Act of 1996 (HIPAA) (Pub L 104–191, 110 Stat 1936).
[6] The Omnibus Rule becomes effective on March 26, 2013, and HIPAA covered entities and business associates must comply with its requirements by September 23, 2013 (the "Compliance Date").

Further, the HIPAA enforcement division for HHS – the Office of Civil Rights (OCR) – has been criticized for not doing enough to enforce the Security Rule provisions of HIPAA[7]. That has all changed with the new imposition of fines that can reach a limit of $1,500,000[8].

Federal Law (HIPAA)   Codified into regulations (Rules)

HIPAA REGULATIONS

There is a huge library of documents known as the **Code of Federal Regulations (C.F.R.)**. Every regulation of the U.S. federal government is codified in the **C.F.R.** -- including the HIPAA **Privacy, Security** and **Data Breach Rules**.

Title 45 of the C.F.R. is the part of the regulations that contains sections addressing HHS. Sub-sections address HIPAA rules. Sections are used to divide up the myriad of regulations into relevant pieces.

---

[7] https://oig.hhs.gov/oas/reports/region4/41105025.pdf
[8] Some of the largest breaches reported to HHS have involved business associates. Penalties are increased for noncompliance based on the level of negligence with a maximum penalty of $1.5 million per violation. The changes also strengthen the Health Information Technology for Economic and Clinical Health (HITECH) Breach Notification requirements by clarifying when breaches of unsecured health information must be reported to HHS.
http://www.hhs.gov/news/press/2013pres/01/20130117b.html

The three major sections of the HIPAA regulations that impact almost all CE/BA organizations are displayed below (the Enforcement Rule authorizes HHS OCR to levy fines and sanctions).

PRIVACY RULE	SECURITY RULE	DATA BREACH NOTIFICATION RULE
45 CFR Part 160 - GENERAL ADMINISTRATIVE REQUIREMENTS 45 CFR Part 164, Subpart A and E - Privacy of Individually Identifiable Health Information	45 CFR Part 164, Subpart C - Security Standards	45 CFR Part 164, Subpart D - Notification in the Case of Breach of Unsecured Protected Health Information

PRIVACY RULE

The Privacy Rule can be thought of as *"the **why** we do things to protect patient privacy"*. Some scholars legitimately believe that the **Privacy Rule** can trace its origins back thousands of years to the beginning of the sacred right of privacy between a patient and a physician[9].

An exhaustive history of the **Privacy Rule** is considered beyond the scope of this booklet. However, the reader should be familiar with the location of Privacy Rule documents that can be obtained at the HHS OCR website (see below):

---

[9] For general privacy information (not HIPAA specific) visit: https://www.privacyassociation.org/

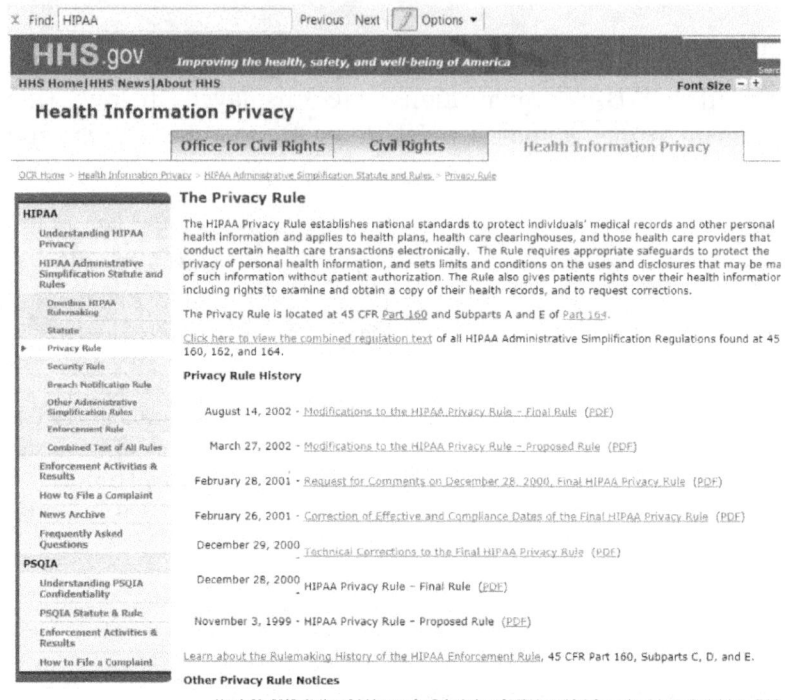

http://www.hhs.gov/ocr/privacy/hipaa/administrative/privacyrule/

Not to oversimplify; but, for the purposes of this booklet the reader should think of the Privacy Rule as addressing the "soft" or "non-technical" concerns of HIPAA.

The Privacy Rule is codified in two major sections within Title 45 of the **C.F.R., Part 160** and **Part 164**. For the novice, understanding these sections will undoubtedly appear a very daunting task. Therefore, subsequent chapters have broken down the Privacy Rule requirements into layman's terms with practical advice on how to comply with the requirements.

It may be a generalization; but, for the purposes instruction, the novice should think of the Privacy Rule as those practices that address paper-based health records and associated organizational practices to protect them. In later chapters there will be more detailed discussion of the types of Protected Health Information (**P.H.I.**).

SECURITY RULE

In contrast, the Security Rule addresses – for the most part – the technical components of protecting **electronic Protected Health Information (e-PHI)**. The novice can think of the Security Rule as "*the **how** we do things to protect patient privacy*".

The Security Rule is located at 45 CFR Part 160 and Subparts A and C of Part 164.

Pictured below is the web-site of HHS addressing the Security Rule. Again, the reader should have a general familiarity with the resources available from the HHS OCR web-site.

http://www.hhs.gov/ocr/privacy/hipaa/administrative/securityrule/

In general terms, the Security Rule will require the lion's share of documentation and evidence that demonstrates e-PHI has been adequately protected and available for proper use.

Safeguards required by the Security Rule will be discussed in later chapters. Suffice to say that there are three major categories of safeguards: (1) Physical, (2) Administrative and (3) Technical.

SECURITY RULE		
PHYSICAL SAFEGUARDS	**ADMINISTRATIVE SAFEGUARDS**	**TECHNICAL SAFEGUARDS**

In general terms, the HIPAA Security Rule addresses the **required** and **addressable** business processes and safeguards needed to ensure **Confidentiality, Integrity and Availability (C.I.A.)** of medical information[10] (paper-based or electronic). This will be addressed in more detail later in this booklet.

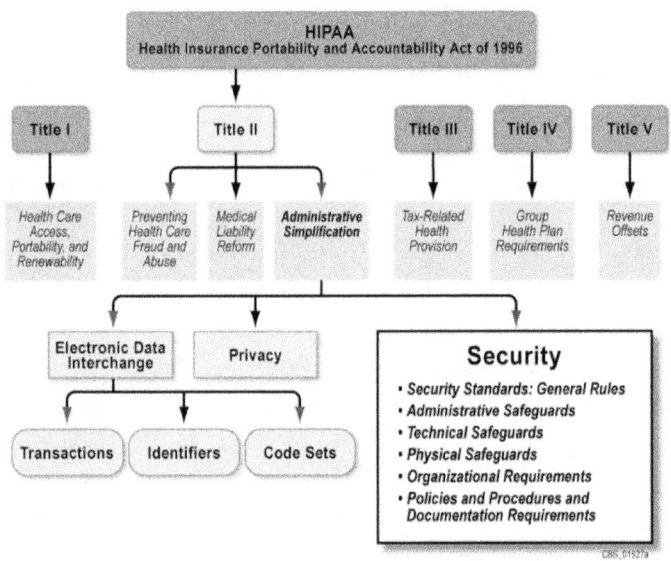

See Special Publication 800-66 of the U.S. National Institute of Standards and Technology (NIST) [discussed in later chapters]

---

[10] Medical Information can be used as a term of art pursuant to the California Confidential Medical Information Act (CMIA). See California Civil Code § 56 et seq.

DATA BREACH NOTIFICATION RULE

A word of caution. As of this writing the President of the United States, in his State of the Union address, has proposed a national data breach notification law. Additionally, there are many individual state data breach notification laws. Although this booklet addresses the HIPAA Breach Notification Rule (45 CFR §§ 164.400-414) it would be prudent to verify local laws in this area.

Pictured below is the HHS OCR Breach Notification Rule web-page. It might be wise to bookmark this browser page.

http://www.hhs.gov/ocr/privacy/hipaa/administrative/breachnotificationrule/

SUMMARY

This chapter introduced the regulatory framework for the HIPAA Privacy, Security and Data Breach Rules (noting that the Enforcement Rule is more aptly applied to the investigative and enforcement powers of the HHS OCR – and may not be that helpful to the reader at this point). The over-arching framework of federal law and implementing agency regulations was explained. The safeguard categories of the HIPAA Security Rule were briefly touched upon.

II. LIABILITY

Each increase in regulatory and technical complexity pushes organizations -- that process, transmit or store protected medical information – a little closer to the possibility that one of the wheels of the machine will break and expose **personally identifiable information** (P.I.I.)[11].

The Anthem data breach (February 2015) – resulting in the compromise of 80 million records -- brought three (3) mass tort class action lawsuits within days of the breach announcement. 11 (eleven) State Attorney Generals have released press statements that they will be investigating Anthem.

As seen in recent civil legal cases, the courts continue to rely on the **HIPAA Privacy and Security Rules** as the *de facto* baseline for measuring due care and reasonableness of an organization's storing, handling, or transmitting of P.I.I.. These **Rules** are the national gold standard to judge the actions of an organization with regards to data protection[12].

---

[11] PII is any information that can directly or indirectly lead to the identification of an individual..

[12] Byrne v. Avery Center for Obstetrics and Gynecology, P.C.,

New HIPAA legal definitions have been codified into federal law (see Omnibus Rule) to describe a state of *"willful neglect"*[13] or the *"conscious, intentional failure or reckless indifference to the obligation to comply"* with regards to complying with these Rules. A finding of "willful neglect" could treble fines and sanctions to $1,500,000 – per incident[14].

Even more troubling, certain parts of the **Privacy Rule** and the entirety of the **Security Rule** may extend to subcontractors of a BA that is contracted to a CE (see also contracted trading partners). Thus, if the "daisy chained" subcontractor (twice removed from the CE) experiences an incident exposing the data that has been entrusted to them, the CE and BA may now be held responsible for the ineffectual monitoring of such subcontractors.

As a a warning to the community, HHS OCR has openly stated that BA audits can be scheduled based upon pure random chance. Industry news reports indicate that federal auditors may compile lists of BAs from a corresponding CE and randomly pick an organization from that list to audit.

NOTE: complaints to the HHS OCR whistleblower hot-line or web-page complaint form may also lead to audit activity and follow-up investigations.

2014 WL 5507439 (Conn. Nov. 11, 2014)
[13] 45 C.F.R. § 160.401
[14] Some of the largest breaches reported to HHS have involved business associates. Penalties are increased for noncompliance based on the level of negligence with a maximum penalty of $1.5 million per violation. The changes also strengthen the Health Information Technology for Economic and Clinical Health (HITECH) Breach Notification requirements by clarifying when breaches of unsecured health information must be reported to HHS.
http://www.hhs.gov/news/press/2013pres/01/20130117b.html

HITECH/ARRA UPDATES

The Health Information Technology for Economic and Clinical Health Act (HITECH) section of the American Recovery and Reinvestment Act (ARRA) of 2009 extended patient rights to access within the HIPAA Privacy Rule.

These new HITECH/ARRA provisions provided that individuals have the right to:

- Obtain copies of their health records (inspection); and,
- Request increased privacy protections; and,
- Amend, or modify, their health information; and,
- Receive a Notice of Privacy Practices (NPP) that outlines how their medical information may be used; and,
- Obtain a record of disclosures of their medical information; and,
- Request copies of electronic Protected Health Information (e-PHI).

Organizations need to address these new requirements in the sensitive area of patient access and patient rights – or, in the alternative, face expensive litigation.

EXAMPLE: Imagine a teenage girl is sexually assaulted when she is 17 y.o. and endures post incident traumatic stress. She may have had several weeks of counseling and received a prescription for anti-depressant drugs. Years later she has graduated from college and is seeking a physician's exam for a new job. She may contact the CE/BA that maintains the treatment records from her teenage experience and request that such records not be released. The CE/BA refuse to amend the records (as they have no policy to address such situations). The young woman files a complaint with HHS OCR. A follow-up investigation ensues. HHS OCR cites the CE/BA for not have a patient right of access policy and assigns a fine of $75,000 USD.

DEMONSTRATING COMPLIANCE

All of these conditions underscore the imperative to demonstrate compliance with the expansion of the federal HIPAA law. Yet, many companies gamble that they will probably never experience a data breach or van audit from the HHS OCR. So – they reason -- why bother with all the red-tape and paperwork to demonstrate compliance?

When such an organization experiences a data breach, they will rightly suffer audits and investigations that may result in heavy fines, litigation, pay-outs of damages, and sanctions. Such an organization will most likely go out of business shortly thereafter.

SUMMARY

Successful demonstration of compliance activities, that showcase actual attempts to comply with these rules, can literally make the difference in determining whether or not the institution should pay several hundred thousands of dollars in damages or fines.

III. AUDIT READINESS

This chapter is designed to help to teach the pupil how to organize and implement HIPAA compliance and data governance activities that will **demonstrate** the reasonable care of an organization in protecting sensitive data, such as P.I.I.

With proper motivation, the reader will discover that a compliance program can be implemented that creates the necessary materials that will demonstrate the reasonable care taken to protect patient medical information.

The purpose of this chapter is to help the reader understand the various "moving parts" of an effective compliance program and to assist their understanding of the integration of the several parts into an organization so as to effect the demonstration of compliance.

COMPLIANCE

Compliance is often thought of as those activities that are undertaken when no one is looking. In other words, compliance is the hallmark of an honor system.

Demonstrations of compliance are built on evidence. Just as an archeologist pieces together artifacts of an ancient civilization, a compliance auditor is trying to piece together a complete picture of how an organization treats the medical information[15] entrusted to it.

Management may not be too concerned about documenting compliance activities until some catastrophic event occurs and the minute details of compliance evidence (or the lack thereof) will be scrutinized for a lapse in reasonable care and possibly a "willful neglect" determination with subsequent treble fines (to the potential of $1,500,000 USD).

Take the airline industry for example. It is assumed by government regulators that well documented procedures will be followed and adhered to by professional and well-meaning personnel to protect passenger safety.

In a catastrophic event (such as an aircraft crash) every scrap of documentation leading up to the crash will undergo a rigorous review against yardsticks of best industry practices, standards, government regulations and laws so that independent accident investigators can understood what exactly happened.

---

[15] At times the author will use the term "medical information". This is a term of art as codified within the California Confidentiality Medical Information Act (CMIA). See California Civil Code § 56.

Unfortunately, for many institutions entrusted with medical information, management may not be too concerned about documenting HIPAA compliance activities until HHS OCR randomly requests the pleasure of reviewing it.

Imagine that the HHS OCR auditors are archeologists or aircraft investigators. They will form an opinion about the organization's reasonable due care given to medical information only by reviewing documentation. This documentation review will take place in a red-tape vacuum. No phone calls, no site visits, no WebEx video seminars – just documentation. No documentation means no reasonable care. Period.

It is the job of the HIPAA audit or compliance practitioner to ensure appropriate materials are prepared and organized in advance of an official audit or lawsuit discovery request

NOTE: HHS OCR will allow only ten (10) days for the response package to be forwarded to their office). For many, that ten (10) day period will begin with a feeling of dread and panic, followed by a burst of activity to comply and finally culminating in finger-pointing, fault-finding, resume updating and job seeking. All preventable.

AUDIT READINESS FOLDER (ARF)

There will be several references to an Audit Readiness Folder (ARF) in the following chapters. An ARF is a folder that contains the documents that demonstrate compliance. It is the final presentation of the hard work that has been undertaken to demonstrate that the institution takes HIPAA/HITECH data governance and compliance activities seriously.

It is suggested that a HIPAA/HITECH ARF be created on a corporate network share drive to allow for the archiving of those documents that will be described in this booklet. Sub-dividing the ARF to align with the HIPAA regulations will align individual folders with the specific rules.

Organizing these materials now will avoid embarrassing delays and missteps when outsiders are seeking records of HIPAA compliance.

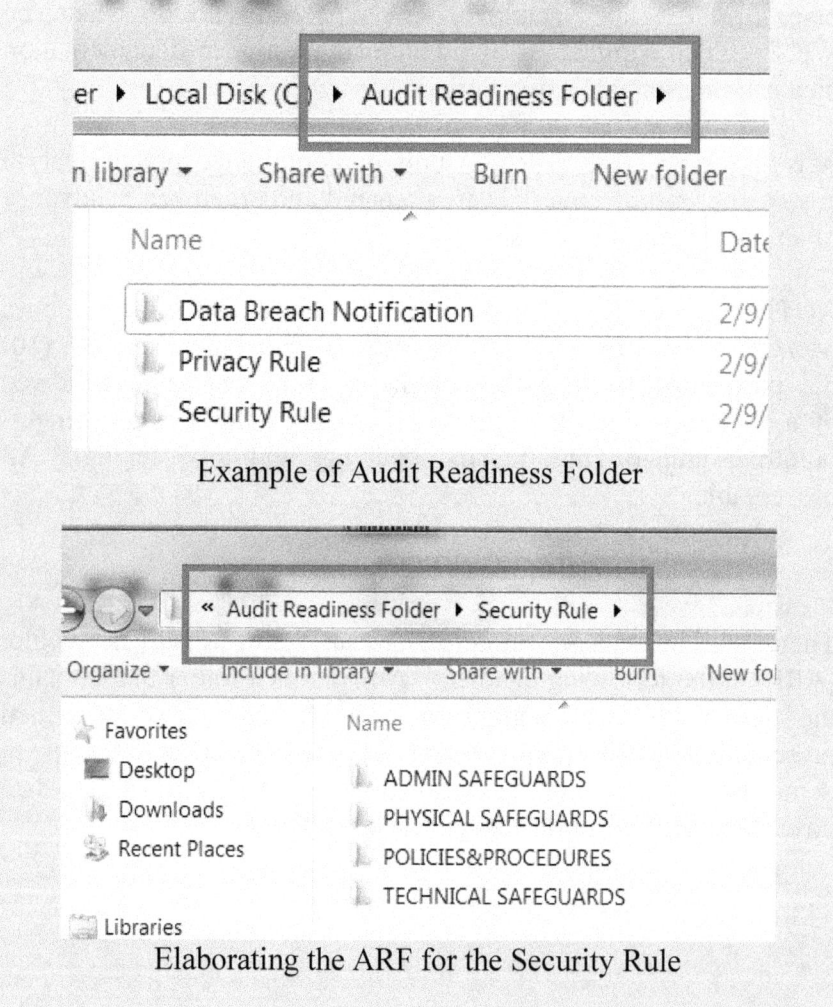

Example of Audit Readiness Folder

Elaborating the ARF for the Security Rule

WORDS OF CAUTION

In the case of a HHS OCR desk audit, auditors will not be taking a tour of the data processing facility and marveling at anti-virus devices, firewalls, new public key infrastructure and other such technical gadgets. They may simply request copies of all the compliance documents used to administer the HIPAA compliance program.

DISCLAIMER

The reader should keep in mind that the regulatory subject matter of the HIPAA federal law can be dry. So. in an effort to make this material more interesting, the author may use hypothetical examples and illustrations to set the tone for the HIPAA practitioner. Although the author may use humor -- at times -- to break up the dry nature of such regulatory subject matter, HIPAA compliance is still serious business. Substantial fines -- even criminal jail terms -- can result in breaches of HIPAA compliance and malicious activities. Although a humorous example may be given, the reader should not misinterpret the author's intent to address this serious topic.

The reader should keep in mind, that without comprehensive training in the fields of information security, auditing, project management and organizational development, etc. many mistakes can be made by a novice. The goal of this booklet is to guide the novice to an appropriate level of detail concerning an overall compliance program.

The reader is cautioned not to exceed the general scope of organizing and facilitating activities described herein. Seek help and assistance when things appear confusing and difficult. Stand in the shoes of a coach and an advisor rather than a subject matter expert (**S.M.E.**).

SUMMARY

This chapter laid the practical ground work for implementing the practical steps in demonstrating compliance. The chapter underscored the importance of appropriate documentation to demonstrate compliance. Suggestions were given on how to organize such documentation in preparation for an audit or investigation.

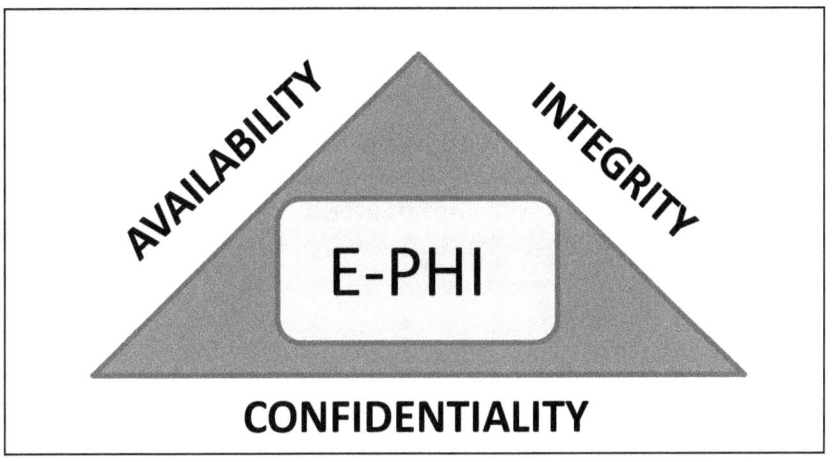

IV. C.I.A.

Thanks to the plethora of spy films and novels the reader should not have any trouble remembering this acronym: **C.I.A.** Within the context of the Security Rule, C.I.A. is the fundamental concept that stands for **Confidentiality, Integrity and Availability (C.I.A.)** with regards to protecting patient privacy.

HHS takes the C.I.A. definition very seriously and applies this term nearly in a universal manner in the context of protecting medical information and personal data that has been entrusted to organizations.

For example, as used in the HIPAA Security Rule:

§ 164.308 (a)(1)(ii)(A)

> *Risk analysis* (Required). Conduct an accurate and
> thorough assessment of the potential risks and
> vulnerabilities to **the confidentiality, integrity, and
> availability** of **electronic protected health information**
> held by the covered entity.

CONFIDENTIALITY	Describes the secrecy of sensitive data. Protecting such data from exposure. Not allowing unauthorized parties to view such data.
INTEGRITY	Describes protection from unauthorized alteration, deletion, modification. Flawed data. Corrupted data.
AVAILABILITY	Describes the availability of data. Critical data available during power black-outs. "Break the glass" emergency situations. Timely access to data.

ELECTRONIC PROTECTED HEALTH INFORMATION

The reader will notice the term "e-PHI" when examining the definition of C.I.A. at the HHS OCR web-site[16];

General Rules

- The Security Rule requires covered entities to maintain reasonable and appropriate administrative, technical, and physical safeguards for protecting e-PHI.

  Specifically, covered entities must:

  1. Ensure the confidentiality, integrity, and availability of all e-PHI they create, receive, maintain or transmit;
  2. Identify and protect against reasonably anticipated threats to the security or integrity of the information;
  3. Protect against reasonably anticipated, impermissible uses or disclosures; and
  4. Ensure compliance by their workforce.[4]

http://www.hhs.gov/ocr/privacy/hipaa/understanding/srsummary.html

Electronic Protected Health Information (**e-PHI**) is defined as:

---

[16] The Security Rule requires covered entities to maintain reasonable and appropriate administrative, technical, and physical safeguards for protecting e-PHI.

Specifically, covered entities must:

1. Ensure the confidentiality, integrity, and availability of all e-PHI they create, receive, maintain or transmit;
2. Identify and protect against reasonably anticipated threats to the security or integrity of the information;
3. Protect against reasonably anticipated, impermissible uses or disclosures; and
4. Ensure compliance by their workforce.

§ 160.103 Definitions.

Electronic protected health information means information that comes within paragraphs (1)(i) or (1)(ii) of the definition of *protected health information* as specified in this section.

Protected Health Information (**PHI**) is defined as:

Protected health information means individually identifiable health information:

Except as provided in paragraph (2) of this definition, that is:
(**i**) Transmitted by electronic media;
(**ii**) Maintained in electronic media; or
(**iii**) Transmitted or maintained in any other form or medium.

Restated, **PHI** is generally considered paper-based health records, while **e-PHI** is the electronic equivalent. The HIPAA Privacy and Security Rules require both forms of information to be protected.

Protecting the secrecy and **confidentiality**, while ensuring the data is not modified in an unauthorized manner (retaining its **integrity**), and ensuring the data is readily **available** for use by authorized parties is the objective of C.I.A[17].

---

[17]

http://www.hhs.gov/ocr/privacy/hipaa/understanding/srsummary.html

TYPES OF MEDIUMS	
Protected Health Information (PHI)	Documents, paper-based artifacts, medical charts, ambulance patient records, treatment records (paper), etc.
Electronic PHI	Bulk data, transmitted medical information, online billing systems, web-site subscriber information, etc.

Sample HHS OCR questions:

§ 164.316	Has the organization documented and implemented a policy for terminating access when a workforce member resigns, is terminated, suspended, retires or access is no longer needed? (CONFIDENTIALITY)
§ 164.312(e)(1)	Does the organization have a process/mechanism to encrypt and decrypt ePHI? (INTEGRITY)
§ 164.310(a)(2)(i)	Does the operational Contingency Plan outline/assign those critical services that must be maintained/restored within specific timeframes? (AVAILABILITY)

DESIGNATED RECORD SET

As a preliminary matter, the entity (BA or CE) needs to determine what medical information is contained in the Designated Record Set (DRS) maintained by the organization that requires C.I.A. protection.

These are records typically used to make decisions about a patient's health care. HHS defines a DRS as:

§ 164.501 Definitions.
As used in this subpart, the following terms have the following meanings:

Designated record set means:

(1) A group of records maintained by or for a covered entity that is:
(i) The medical records and billing records about individuals maintained by or for a covered health care provider;
(ii) The enrollment, payment, claims adjudication, and case or medical management record systems maintained by or for a health plan; or
(iii) Used, in whole or in part, by or for the covered entity to make decisions about individuals.
(2) For purposes of this paragraph, the term record means any item, collection, or grouping of information that includes protected health information and is maintained, collected, used, or disseminated by or for a covered entity.
Direct treatment relationship means a treatment relationship between an individual and a health care provider that is not an indirect treatment relationship.

The key to the DRS is that it is groups of files or groups of records. These groups may import individual pieces of PII[18] into the group, which may extend Privacy Rule protections to the entire group of records.

Examples of Designated Record Sets
Enrollment – Payment – Claims adjudication
Patients accounts folder
Case management records

Sample audit question:

§164.528	Has the organization documented and implemented a Designated Record Set (DRS)?

SUMMARY

This chapter introduced the C.I.A. triad: confidentiality, integrity and availability. The C.I.A. triad will be applied to many of the discussions related to appropriate safeguards to protect medical information. A real-world example of a data record set (DRS) was presented so the reader could apply the C.I.A. concept to a tangible component of the enterprise (database, groups of files, etc.).

---

[18] Personally identifiable information (PII)

Dave Sweigert

REALITY CHECK

V. AUTHORITY TO PROMOTE CHANGE

§ 164.530(a)   Personnel Designations -

1. *Standard: personnel designations.*
   i.   A covered entity must designate a privacy official who is responsible for the development and implementation of the policies and procedures of the entity.

Notice the words "implementation" in the above citation. Chances are, that an individual person may not have sufficient clout to effect change in an organization. The HIPAA Privacy Officer will need to understand certain realities of organizational behavior, organizational development and change to be successful.

ORGANIZATIONAL FRAMEWORK

An organizational framework can extend the reach of the HIPAA practitioner's influence by leveraging activities of a working group, task force, special committee, etc.

The characteristics of a successful framework will include how the group develops appropriate action plans that lead to the implementation of HIPAA components. For instance, such a framework (committee, working group) may be comprised of the HIPAA Privacy Officer, General Counsel, Director of Human Resources, Director of I.T., etc. Membership is not as important as an action focus.

Facilitated workshops offer a method to keep small groups focused on achievable outcomes. Tools are available for defining achievable objectives.

In the mid-1980's a term known as "Quality Circles" was all the rage in the manufacturing industry. Quality Circles embodied the idea of a multi-player participatory process that fostered open communications to improve processes in the organization. This was part of a movement known as "Organizational Development" ("O.D.").

O.D. fostered the concept of maturing organizational activities to create more effective processes and procedures to improve the quality of output and product. O.D. coined the term "change agent" to describe an individual that would help facilitate process improvement for the overall benefit of the entire institution.

In many ways the HIPAA practitioner is such a change agent and will work (coaching/advising) with departments to foster the ability to demonstrate compliance.

Newly appointed HIPAA practitioners will soon discover that there will be a honeymoon period where most organizations will breathe a sigh of relief that there is now a name in the blank check box on the HIPAA compliance audit form. This state of euphoria will soon begin to dissipate when the new Privacy Officer begins asking line managers to create procedures that support the compliance program.

This is usually when the institutional resistance and push-back can begin. Sometimes it can be ugly and unprofessional. Line managers are not above personal attacks and crude jokes that will mock the HIPAA compliance program. This is where an organizational framework may help.

It will be much easier to elicit cooperation from a group than an individual manager. Especially, if the group perceives that many hands will make the work light. If the new Privacy Officer can structure the organizational compliance framework in such a way as to mimic the participatory style of quality circle that may help create a sense of participation with the compliance program.

This may require what O.D. practitioners refer to as "reverent authority". Although the practitioner may lack direct line authority, his/her authority as a subject matter expert (SME) in the world of HIPAA compliance makes them the expert.

By adopting a coaching or advisory mindset, this expert may be perceived as a non-threatening change agent simply attempting to facilitate a positive change in the organization, based on their overall individual expert knowledge.

Within the O.D. context, formal authority (or real authority) is the right to decide -- authority the expert may not have. The HIPAA expert's goal is to integrate those individuals with real authority (or their representatives) into the HIPAA quality circle process and leverage their authority.

Be prepared to seek assistance from members of the HIPAA quality circle in the areas of planning for compliance, organizing compliance activities, staffing or resource allocation for HIPAA activities, how compliance efforts will be directed, who will be controlling the overall outcome of HIPAA compliance, etc.

For the purposes of this booklet, the assumption is made that the HIPAA expert will have informal authority in such a group. Therefore, they will be looked upon as the HIPAA SME to help the group establish common goals and objectives. This can be done by centering discussions around common core values and objectives (doing what's best for the patient, delivering quality service to our customer, etc.). Keeping discussions focused on goal-oriented outcomes and avoiding debates and the "let me correct you" discussions.

In the adviser role, the expert is helping the group to use its resources to support the group's compliance goals. The HIPAA practitioner can facilitate discussions in a non-threatening and consequence free environment that fosters open communications and sharing, while acting as the compliance expert to help the group understand the institution's duties and responsibilities under HIPAA.

Keep in mind that the other group members have other responsibilities and duties in the organization. They may have a few hours a month to devote to assisting with the HIPAA quality circle or compliance committee.

The practitioner's task is to leverage the group dynamics of the HIPAA quality circle and not waste people's time. The goal of the HIPAA framework is to provide a means to assimilate HIPAA compliance objectives into the organization's processes (albeit formal and informal). Achieving "buy-in" for tactical "baby steps" might be the first goal -- after all, one has to crawl before one can walk.

SMART OBJECTIVES

A management tool that helps small groups in setting achievable objectives and goals is known as the S.M.A.R.T. method. This method helps facilitators of small groups to develop Specific, Measurable, Attainable, Realistic and Time objectives that can be rolled into action plans.

S = Specific

M = Measurable

A = Attainable

R = Realistic

T = Timely

The S.M.A.R.T. Methodology[19]

Smart	Use specific terms, avoid vague abstracts
Measurable	Method to objectively measuring success
Achievable	Are challenging but realistic
Relevant	Follow the business strategy of the organization
Timely	Specify a time period

How to define SMART objectives

---

[19] See National Fire Academy (NFA).

PROJECT CHARTER

It may be advisable to consider a "Project Charter" to serve as a foundational document to provide a sense of authority and authenticity to the HIPAA quality circle or other committee.

The project charter concept is normally associated with self-contained tangible products that are not just process improvement activities. Depending on the state of the organization's HIPAA compliance, a project charter may be appropriate if a big task is before the HIPAA practitioner.

A project charter is essentially a foundation contract between stakeholders and the project manager. The charter appoints a project manager in writing and provides that individual with a certain level of authority.

Stakeholders may include the Board of Trustees, Board of Directors, senior leadership, line managers, customers, patients, etc. In sum, the undertaking of HIPAA compliance is to serve the desires of the stakeholders. For instance, the Board would certainly not desire headlines about their institution's data breach and subsequent civil lawsuits.

The project charter will outline assumptions and expected results. Assumptions may be constraints forced upon the HIPAA practitioner. For instance, perhaps senior leadership demands that HIPAA compliance activities do not interfere with normal business operations. Constraints might include budgets, deadlines, reporting and notifications (perhaps a quarterly report to the Board is required, etc.).

There are many resources available that can guide the practitioner concerning the creation of a project charter[20].

---

[20] http://www.pmi.org/

SUMMARY

This chapter touched on the role of the privacy practitioner in a HIPAA/HITECH regulated entity. Tools and techniques were explained that may assist the privacy practitioner in building a culture of compliance within the organization.

VI.   RED FLAG WARNINGS

Many documents and work products are easily accessible by the public – and by default HHS OCR. This is especially true concerning materials on web-sties operated by CEs, BAs and impacted trading partners, etc.

A public statement that contains errors and omissions can be very problematic for an institution. Inaccurate documents can increase the observer's level of doubt concerning the competency of the organization to protect medical information.

In other words, these are "RED FLAGS" to the healthcare compliance community, indicating that the organization "flying" such red flags may have a very weak understanding of HIPAA and associated rules.

For the purposes of instruction, the reader will be exposed to several RED FLAG warnings in this chapter that cry out for attention. Regrettably, an exhaustive analysis cannot be conducted on each and every red flag issue. But, this booklet will address these sample concerns and provide methodologies that will guide the reader to further investigate corrective actions.

NOTE: Once updated, these pieces of evidence (**artifacts**) will be pre-positioned in an **audit readiness file** (**ARF**) to be given to auditors. Building out a complete and comprehensive **ARF** is the end-game and addressed in more detail in subsequent chapters.

RED FLAG: PRIVACY OFFICER NOT APPOINTED IN WRITING

Appointing a Privacy Official in writing is required by § 164.530; see "ADMINISTRATIVE REQUIREMENTS"[21].

---

[21] § 164.530 Administrative requirements.

(a)

(1) *Standard: Personnel designations.*

(i) A covered entity must designate a **privacy official** who is responsible for the development and implementation of the policies and procedures of the entity.

(ii) A covered entity must designate a contact person or office who is responsible for receiving complaints under this section and who is able to provide further information about matters covered by the notice required by § 164.520.

(2) *Implementation specification: Personnel designations.* A covered entity **must document the personnel designations** in paragraph (a)(1) of this section as required by paragraph (j) of this section.

The simple act of obtaining a written piece[22] of paper, that appoints an individual as the Privacy Official, is the first step in building out the **ARF** for the compliance program to be audit ready. It would be a prudent idea for the HIPAA audit practitioner to have an electronic copy of this document in the ARF (as well as paper-based) in a physical ARF.

RED FLAG: MISALIGNED NPP

The **Notice of Privacy Practices (NPP)** is a semi-publicly available document that outlines the organization's practices with regards to handling medical information, allowing for notification to patients, etc.[23]

A list of qualifying questions is provided in Annex A to help the HIPAA compliance practitioner assess the validity of the organization's NPP.

Sample HHS OCR audit question:

§164.520, §164.520(b)(1)	Is the Notice of Privacy Practices (NPP) posted in a prominent location visible to clients? If, applicable, where is the NPP posted?

§ 164.520(b)	Does the NPP match the description of the organization's processes and procedures regarding accounting of disclosures, complaint resolution, access, denial of access or addition/amendments, etc.?

[23] § 164.520 **Notice of privacy practices** for protected health information.
(a) *Standard: notice of privacy practices—*
(1) *Right to notice.* Except as provided by paragraph (a)(2) or (3) of this section, an individual has a right to adequate notice of the uses and disclosures of protected health information that may be made by the covered entity, and of the individual's rights and the covered entity's legal duties with respect to protected health information.

NOTE: the NPP must accurately describe – for the patient (in their language) – patient rights to access Protected Health Information (PHI)[24].

§164.520(b)	Has the NPP been revised, amended or updated since the publication of the Final Omnibus Rule (see HIPAA Omnibus Rule, Jan. 17, 2013)?

NOTE: The NPP should be reviewed against § 164.520[25])(b) *"Implementation specifications: content of notice"*. It is wise to keep notes about how the organization ensured the NPP met the criteria of the implementation specifications that define content.

Other NPP "gotchas":

- Both paper and electronic NPPs do not match in content and effective date

- CE or BA maintains a website, but the NPP is not posted on that website

- NPP forms are only available in English

- NPPs are not changed after there is a material change to practices addressed in the NPP

- No statement as to the right to breach notification

---

[24] There are several terms of art for sensitive information. The California Medical Information Act (CMIA) refers to "medical information". The HIPAA Privacy and Security Rules refer to PHI and electronic PHI (e-PHI).
[25] For day to day reference to HIPAA it is appropriate to drop the 45 C.F.R. and rely on the Section symbol. Example: § 164.520

- No contact information for Privacy Official

- Caveat: The rules on distributing revised NPPs are different for health care providers and health plans

RED FLAG: MISALIGNED BREACH POLICIES

The Omnibus Rule specifically modified the **Breach Notification Rule** which creates a presumption that unauthorized disclosure of PHI constitutes a data breach, unless a risk assessment of the incident concludes otherwise.

Four new risk factors are required to be evaluated as part of the data breach risk assessment:

- Nature and extent of PHI involved

- The unauthorized person who used the PHI or to whom the disclosure was made

- Whether the PHI actually was acquired or viewed

- The extent to which the risk to the PHI has been mitigated

Institutional data breach policies and/or procedures (discussed if subsequent chapters) should demonstrate that they have been updated with such material changes in the law, rule or regulation.

Important thresholds that trigger notifications in the event of a data breach remain unchanged, such as: (1) if **500** or more health records have been breached (exposed to unauthorized third parties) HHS OCR must be advised of same within (2) sixty **(60)** days (amongst other required activities).

These rules also require notification to the individuals whose records may have been breached. An annual report is also submitted of data breaches below the 500 individual record threshold. Data breach notification rules are designed to provide consumers (in this case patients) adequate notice that their PHI or e-PHI may have been compromised (e-PHI refers to electronic copies of PHI)[26].

NOTE: In California, depending on the organization's status as a health care provider, notification may be required to the **California Department of Public Health** (CDPH) within 15 days of a breach -- as well as to the HHS 45 days later. For instance, if data operations occur in Kansas, the database may still contain the records of Californians. If a breach occurs involving over 500 records of Californians the organization may be obligated to notify authorities in California.

Any updates to the data breach policies or procedures should be made to bring them current with the Omnibus Rule.

HHS OCR auditors will want to see evidence (remember -- demonstrating compliance) that the organization took the possibility of a data breach seriously and is tracking changes in the law and updated policies accordingly.

---

[26] In theory, after a data breach notification the consumer is now equipped with the information he/she needs to monitor their credit report for any unorthodox activity that would indicate identity thieves have used the breach data to obtain credit cards and the like.

NOTE: at some point it would be advisable for an institution to build a cross-domain inter-departmental team that will be convened if there is a suspected data breach. This may involve I.T. security, legal advisor, human resources, public affairs (Public Information Officer (P.I.O.)), etc. The team concept is addressed in later chapters. Document team meetings and any table top exercises (TTXs) to help train the team in data breach mitigation techniques.

It is advisable for the institution's **updated**[27] data breach notification policy to describe the roles and responsibilities of team members on the data breach management team.

A WORD ABOUT
ENCRYPTION AND
DATA BREACH NOTIFICATIONS

When there is a purported "data breach" the risk assessment needs to be conducted to determine if a **bona fide** data breach actually occurred. The first determination of such a risk assessment includes the status of the data itself -- whether it was encrypted or unencrypted.

For example, if a bulk data tape drive with eight (8) million e-PHI health records fell off the data truck and said tape was encrypted (or enciphered), then there would be reasonable cause to believe the data has been rendered useless (to unauthorized access).

---

[27] NOTE: Modernizing policies and procedures to reflect the current state of laws and regulations is a HIPAA requirement.

§ 164.530 Administrative requirements.(i)

(3) *Implementation specification: Changes in law.* Whenever there is a change in law that necessitates a change to the covered entity's policies or procedures, the covered entity must promptly document and implement the revised policy or procedure.

Below are questions that should be addressed in the data breach risk assessment (archive copies in the **ARF**). Sample questions to be answered after a data breach is discovered:

- How was it determined there was or was not a Privacy/Security Rule violation or data breach?

- How was it confirmed that the data in question was encrypted?

- Was this just a "good faith" accidental exposure; such as, unintentional acquisition by an employee, inadvertent disclosure to an authorized business partner, incidental exposure to a subcontractor, etc.?

RED FLAG: INCOMPLETE
WORKFORCE TRAINING

HIPAA promotes the term "workforce" as it encompasses employees, temps, subcontractors, etc. Every workforce member that handles **e-PHI/PHI** will need HIPAA awareness training. Documentation that such training was legally sufficient to meet the need of educating the workforce will need to be documented[28].

---

[28] § 164.530 Administrative requirements. (b)
(1) *Standard: Training.* A covered entity must train all members of its workforce on the policies and procedures with respect to protected health information required by this subpart and subpart D of this part, **as necessary and appropriate for the members of the workforce to carry out their functions within the covered entity.**

It should be verified that such workforce training provides the proper definition of PHI[29]. PHI includes 18 identifiers, or attributes, of personal information. Examples of PHI include (not a complete list, some individual attributes combined into a logical category, such as e-mail addresses and I.P. numbers, designated with (C)):

Individual's name
All geographic subdivisions smaller than a State
Dates: including birth date, admission date,, discharge date
Telephone numbers and/or fax numbers (combined)(C)
E-mail addresses and/or Internet Protocol (I.P.) addresses (C)
Social security numbers
Medical record numbers and/or Health plan beneficiary numbers (C)
Vehicle identifiers and serial numbers, including license plate numbers
Biometric identifiers, including finger and voice prints
Full face photographic images and any comparable images
Certificate/license numbers
Account numbers and/or Any other unique identifying number, characteristic, or code

---

[29] Section 1171 of Part C of Subtitle F of Public Law 104-191 (August 21, 1996)

Any combination of the above data types can be considered a PHI record, such as: (1) name, address, e-mail address; or, (2) name, health plan number, photo of patient; or, (3) social security number, date of birth, telephone number, etc.

§ 164.502(a)	**_Standard._** A covered entity or business associate may not use or disclose **protected health information**, except as permitted or required by this subpart or by subpart C of part 160 of this subchapter.

As noted above, the training should address what constitutes authorized disclosures and permitted use.

It is suggested that the Privacy Officer work with Human Resources to see if such HIPAA awareness training is documented in employee (workforce) records. Various on-line training courses offer completion certificates that can be placed into such files. However, be mindful that a representative sample of such materials should also be stored in the ARF.

Implementers of the training policy need to understand where these certificates are located and how they can be quickly gathered up in the event of an audit request.

Although on-line training courses are fine, they are very generic in scope and may not convey the corporate attitude about HIPAA. It may be wise to visit department staff meetings and provide periodic HIPAA updates and briefings (documentation of such briefings with an attendance sheet may be kept with a copy of the course materials in the audit readiness folder).

RED FLAG: NON-EXISTENT OR
SLOPPY SANCTION POLICY

The Sanction Policy is another core basic policy that undoubtedly HHS OCR auditors will want to see and review. The Sanction Policy creates a corporate imperative to require "sanctions[30]" for those workforce members that are involved in a data breach[31].

It is a wise idea to have some employees' behavior recorded as sanctioned so that there is evidence in the ARF.

In other words, a blank folder that shows no sanctionable activity in the last year could indicate a very lax detection method and may increase doubt about the institution's compliance program.

---

[30] **§ 164.530 Administrative requirements (e)**

(1) *Standard: Sanctions.* A covered entity must have and apply appropriate **sanctions against members of its workforce who fail to comply with the privacy policies and procedures** of the covered entity or the requirements of this subpart or subpart D of this part. This standard does not apply to a member of the covered entity's workforce with respect to actions that are covered by and that meet the conditions of § 164.502(j) or paragraph (g)(2) of this section.

(2) *Implementation specification: Documentation.* As required by paragraph (j) of this section, a covered entity must document the sanctions that are applied, if any.

[31] **§ 164.308 Administrative requirements (a)(1)(ii)**

(C) *Sanction policy (Required).* Apply appropriate sanctions against workforce members who fail to comply with the security policies and procedures of the covered entity.

NOTE: Human Resources will most likely want to do an across the board "level set" and ensure that all workforce members are trained to a consistent level (this will serve as a baseline for training). It will then be considered appropriate to identify individuals for remedial training programs for those workforce members that have been involved in a data breach or security incident.

RED FLAG: IMPROPERLY
DEALING WITH WHISTLEBLOWERS

When engaging the workforce in the training process, it is a good time to address HIPAA whistle-blower protections. Hopefully proactive Privacy Officers will be viewed by the workforce as the first person to complain to about perceived violations of the HIPAA Privacy and Security Rules.

The HHS OCR wants to believe that there is the ability for workforce members to have free and open communications with the HHS hotline or web complaint form and they may seek documentation of this.

It may be wise to include information about whistleblower protections in the HIPAA awareness training package. Compliance posters also contain such information (it is wise to take several photographs of such compliance posters and place copies of this pictures in the audit readiness file).

In this era of whistleblower complaints, be prepared to demonstrate a policy or procedure (discussed in the next chapter) that addresses investigations of such complaints.

The HIPAA complaint policy or procedure should describe how to document such complaints and how they will be investigated. Investigative results, memos about resolution or corrective action plans (CAPs) that address the concern should be appropriately stored, archived and copied into your audit readiness folder.

Workforce reminders in training sessions, e-mails, compliance posters, etc. should convey the point that a non-retaliation posture will be taken by the institution when such reports are made to HHS OCR[32].

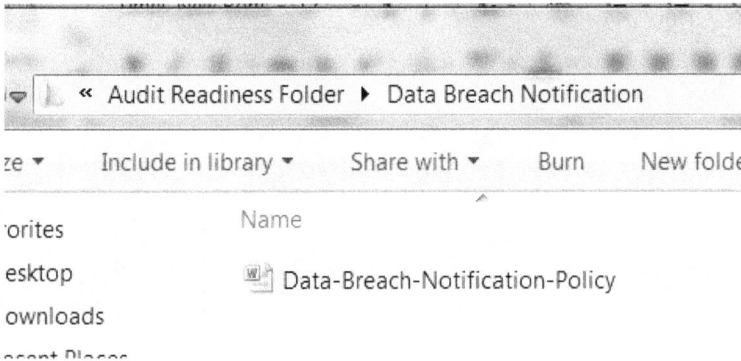

Archiving policy in ARF as part of audit readiness

---

[32] **§ 164.530(g)** *Standard: Refraining from intimidating or retaliatory acts*. A covered entity--

1. May not intimidate, threaten, coerce, discriminate against, or take other retaliatory action against any individual for the exercise by the individual of any right established, or for participation in any process provided for, by this subpart or subpart D of this part, including the filing of a complaint under this section; and
2. Must refrain from intimidation and retaliation as provided in Sec. 160.316 of this subchapter.

SUMMARY

This chapter provided a cross section of typical findings often cited by the HHS OCR. Specific examples were provided of the type of unsatisfactory conditions that might be identified during an audit or investigation.

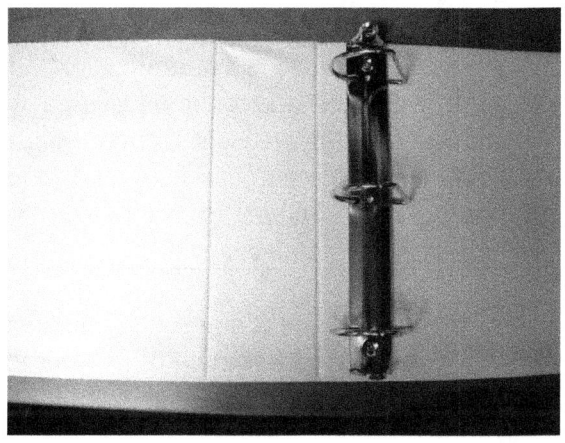

VII.POLICIES & PROCEDURES

The creation of appropriate documentation that is safely retained and stored is a requirement of the HIPAA Security Rule. In fact, the creation of appropriate policies and procedures (P&Ps) is a specific requirement[33].

[33] § 164.316 Policies and procedures and documentation requirements.

A covered entity must, in accordance with § 164.306:(a) *Standard: Policies and procedures.* Implement reasonable and appropriate policies and procedures to comply with the standards, implementation specifications, or other requirements of this subpart, taking into account those factors specified in § 164.306(b)(2)(i), (ii), (iii), and (iv). This standard is not to be construed to permit or excuse an action that violates any other standard, implementation specification, or other requirements of this subpart. A covered entity may change its policies and procedures at any time, provided that the changes are documented and are implemented in accordance with this subpart.

POLICY FRAMEWORK

The policy framework is a tool that includes a process design that indicates how policies will be official approved and distributed. The framework can leverage a committee or working group to spread the responsibilities and duties for implementing HIPAA across organizational inter-departmental and cross-domain boundaries. P&Ps can become unwieldy and unmanageable very quickly; therefore, it is prudent to begin the P&P endeavor by having such a framework in place.

Creating an over-arching numbering scheme for families of similar polices will help with the management of policies in the life-cycle.:

For example:

Overarching Security Policy Framework	01 - Administrative Safeguards
	02 - Physical Safeguards
	03 - Technical Safeguards
	04 - Organizational Safeguards
	05 - Documentation Requirements

Sub-divisions create detailed categories:

02 – Physical Safeguards	02.1 - Facility Access Controls § 164.310(a)(3)
	02.2 - Workstation Use § 164.310(b)
	02.3 - Workstation Security § 164.310©

A policy template can be fashioned to identify each individual policy with an appropriate header, as seen below.

FACILITY ACCESS CONTROLS	
TITLE:	VISITOR CONTROL POLICY
DATE:	MAR 3, 2015
NUMBER:	2005-A-004
APPROVED:	Mark Markenson, V.P. of Compliance
PURPOSE:	This policy has been defined to control the movement of contractors, third parties and other non-workforce members that access the controlled facility.
CITE:	164.310(a)(2)(iii) Standard: Facility access controls – Access control and validation procedures

NOTE: Traditionally, a P&P is considered valid when it is (1) no longer in a draft state, (2) has been formally approved by an authorizing official, (3) and has been dated.

It is wise to build out an inventory list of P&Ps with the final approval date. The example below would be the accurate description of a policy in such an inventory:

Sanction Policy	Issued 6/6/2014	Signed by B. Sims

POLICY DEFINITION

Next, the policy life cycle should be defined to indicate how polices are created, edited, reviewed, analyzed and finally approved. Several models exist; but, in the end the organization will need to experiment and refine a process that works effectively.

Stage one of such a life cycle begins with the initiation of the specific policy. As depicted in the graph below, this will begin with accessing compliance requirements, merging business requirements, drafting the initial policy, and submitting before an approving body (such as a committee), etc.

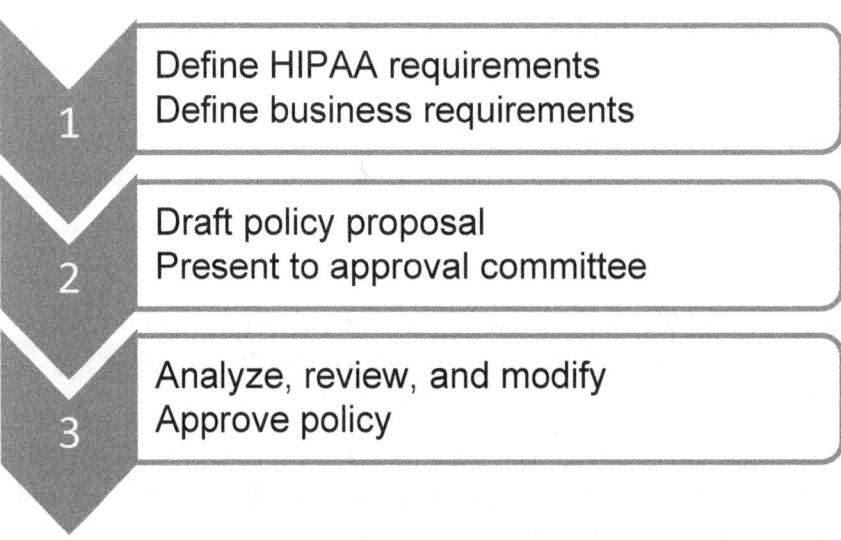

1
Define HIPAA requirements
Define business requirements

2
Draft policy proposal
Present to approval committee

3
Analyze, review, and modify
Approve policy

Example of policy creation process

To prepare for the creation of appropriate audit ready P&Ps one must understand the concept of design evidence. **Design evidence** refers to the state of affairs as they should be, in layman's terms. Think of design evidence as the blueprint for a house, the overarching plan for a new city park, e.g. the "way it should be built" document.

During the policy definition phase (when one begins to create an initial policy) it will be helpful to rely HIPAA regulations. The process/procedure phase will rely on industry best practices.

HIPAA Requirements

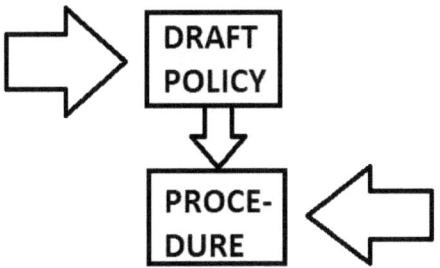

Industry best practice

Example of policy and procedure inputs

Subsequent chapters in this booklet will address an HHS OCR recommended source for best practices, the U.S. National Institute for Standards and Technology (N.I.S.T.).

NOTE: there is a temptation to over-engineer initial polices with gratuitous use of standards to create an idealized vision of the organization's operations.

In essence, the initial policy (which will become design evidence) spelling out the compliance gold standard to which the organization should aspire to.

Sample HHS OCR audit question:

§164.316	Does the organization have written policies relating to HIPAA and state laws privacy and security requirements?

There will be a temptation to throw in kitchen sink best practices into such policy drafts; as if to stuff a suit case so that it is bulging with information. Kitchen sink policies will often quote dozens of national standards and include phrases such as "the organization must employ" or "personnel will be required to do such and such", etc. Caution and prudence must be exercised to sparely use words such as "must" and "required" as they demand strict compliance and leave little room for flexibility.

NOTE: Third parties (auditors, juries, investigators) may not be very sympathetic actual organizational conduct measured against this type of kitchen sink policies. Following an incident (such as a data breach) they may legalistically seek evidence that such policies were indeed enforced. When no such evidence is offered, the level of confidence in such policies making a practical impact on the organization will plummet.

POLICY IMPLEMENTATION

The next phase of the policy life-cycle is the implementation phase. In this stage the policy is communicated to appropriate workforce members that are tasked with enabling the practical implementation of the policy.

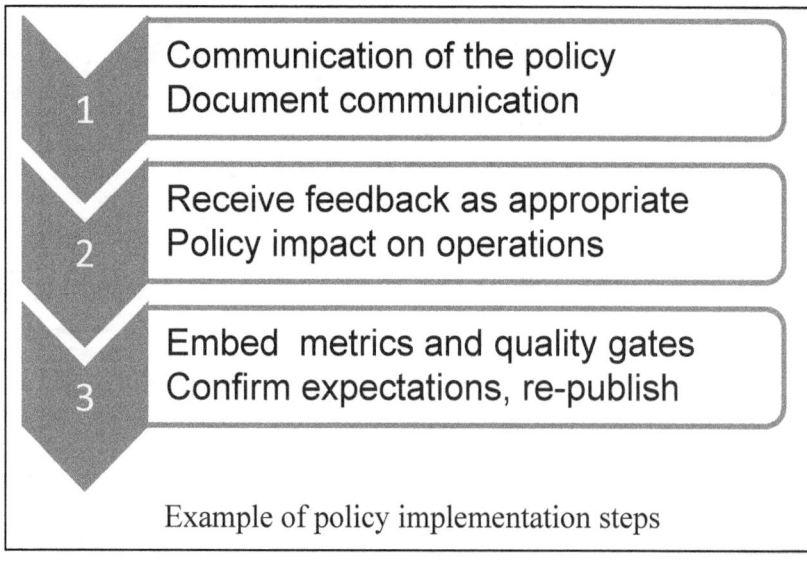

Example of policy implementation steps

During the policy implementation phase it is prudent to meet the pesky cousin of **Design Evidence,** the rouge known as **Operational Evidence**.

Operational Evidence is the "way things really are". The condemned shack is the reality of the majestic blueprint. The hazardous waste storage site is the reality to the city's new plan for a new park. In other words, the larger the reality gap between design evidence and operational evidence, the more the likelihood of increasing doubt in the auditor's mind that the policies have had an effect on the organization.

Metrics are drivers for **Key Performance Indicators** (KPI) that can use a type of "quality gate" to track implementation of a policy. Such "reality checks" can be embedded within policies to help populate metrics and KPIs, facilitating the collection of relevant operational evidence that is created to fulfill the policy requirement. This will become more important in the discussion on risk management and mitigation in subsequent chapters.

For example, the newly created Sanction Policy may have a metric-driven quality gate such as requirement that all workforce members must acknowledge receiving a copy of the policy on a yearly basis. The KPI quality gate may be a sign-up roster available at quarterly staff meetings that specifically states workforce members have acknowledged receiving a copy of the Sanctions Policy.

KPI: Percentage of workforce acknowledging recipient of Sanction Policy			
1st QTR	2nd QTR	3rd QTR	4th QTR
76%	57%	75%	69%

Both types of documents, (1) design evidence (the Sanction Policy itself) with the embedded metric requiring acknowledgements, and (2) the operational evidence (the acknowledgement roster) are auditable artifacts. Together, they both demonstrate compliance with the requirement for a Sanction Policy.

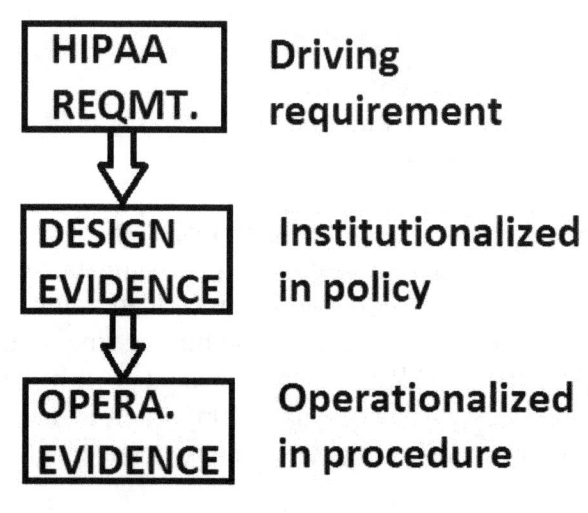

Examples of types of evidence

NOTE: Both types of documents (design evidence and operational evidence) can be archived in an ARF. Discussed in more detail later.

Consideration should be given to organizing a working group to brainstorm practical quality gate metrics that can be embedded with the policies (or procedures – to be discussed later).

SUBMISSION OF ARTIFACTS TO HHS OCR

The concept of the audit readiness folder (ARF) is a mechanism to pre-position evidence that may be requested by OCR HHS. Archiving materials in the ARF, located within relevant categories, will aid in the demonstration of compliance to OCR HHS auditors.

Industry press reports indicate that HHS OCR is preparing a compliance web portal that will accept electronic documents that can uploaded (file transfer) to a compliance portal.

In sum, the ARF will contain all the necessary electronic documents that may be requested as part of an OCR HHS "desk audit". The term "desk audit" was coined by an auditing contractor employed by the Centers for Medicare and Medicaid Services (CMS) conducting compliance audits as part of the Meaningful Use incentive payment program[34].

CAUTION: HHS OCR will allow an "auditee" ten (10) days to submit requested documents (no extensions or requests for elaboration allowed). Avoid thinking that purchasing the $100 quick fix "HIPAA compliant" policy generator will offer a last minute bail-out for responding to a OCR HHS desk audit. HHS OCR will undoubtedly have the ability to validate the meta data of the electronic documents submitted to the compliance portal and to verify if such as evidence has been back dated.

---

[34] CMS is part of HHS. Figliozzi and Company will be performing the meaningful use audits for CMS. If you are selected for an audit you will receive a letter from them with the CMS logo on the letterhead.
https://questions.cms.gov/faq.php?id=5005&faqId=7361

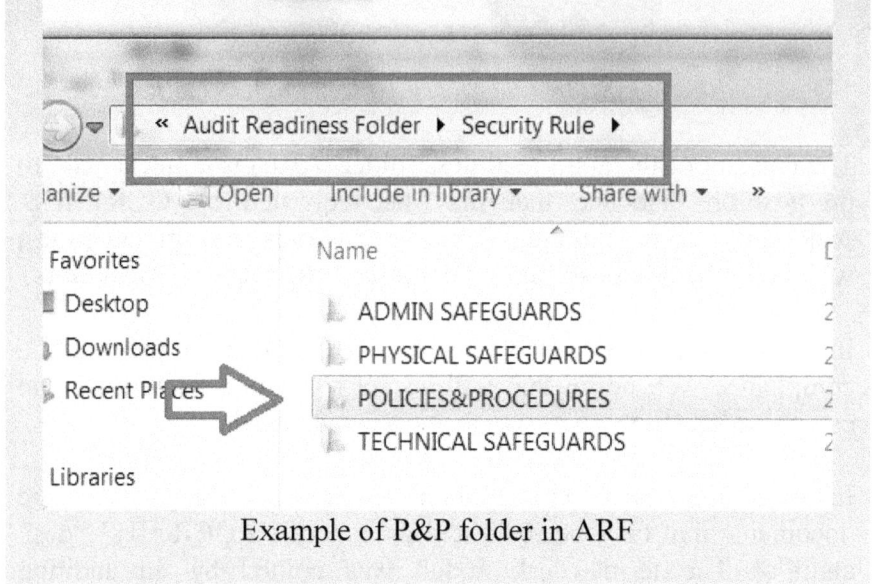

Example of P&P folder in ARF

POLICY DRIVERS

For illustrative purposes, the issue of P&Ps needed for the requirement of patient access to medical information will be addressed here. This illustrates the policy drivers derived from the implementing federal regulations for HIPAA/HITECH.

Included in this section are sample auditor questions that an HHS OCR investigator might ask. These questions are designed as a self-check for the HIPAA/HITECH privacy practitioner.

For example, P&Ps should be in-place that addresses how medical information can be accessed by an individual – or their designated personal representative (PR). A written document should address the process for requesting copies of health records by a patient or their PR.

§ 164.524 Access of individuals to protected health information.
(a) *Standard: Access to protected health information—*
(1) *Right of access.* Except as otherwise provided in paragraph (a)(2) or (a)(3) of this section, an individual has a right of access to inspect and obtain a copy of protected health information about the individual in a designated record set, for as long as the protected health information is maintained in the designated record set,

NOTE: There is a patchwork of state laws that also govern patient medical information. For instance, in California the **Patient Access to Health Records Act (PAHRA)**[35] gives patients the right to inspect and correct their health records (with some exceptions). PAHRA also gives patients the opportunity to correct health records that they believe are inaccurate. It is wise to check with the local state laws when fashioning a patient medical record policy.

Examples of Personal Representative Issues
Parent or guardian (person who has authority to make health care decisions for a minor)
Some state laws may not require PR approval of medical treatment
PR may have to agree to confidentiality between minor and healthcare provider

---

[35] Cal. Health & Safety Code §§ 123100-123149.1

Sample HHS OCR audit question:

§ 164.524(a)	Has the organization documented and implemented a process for individuals to access their health care records or request copies?

Certain types of medical information can be classified as "sensitive" because additional protections apply to such records. "SUPER HIPAA" health records include:

- Mental health records; and,
- Drug and alcohol counseling and treatment; and,
- Records of children and minors; and,
- Reproductive records, contraceptive prescriptions for minors; and,
- Certain criminal and civil artifacts of evidence for courts; and,
- Treatment of AIDS/HIV, sexually transmitted diseases, etc.

§ 164.524 Access of individuals to protected health information.
(a) *Standard: Access to protected health information*—
(1) *Right of access.* . . . .except for [EXEMPTIONS]:
(i) Psychotherapy notes;
(ii) Information compiled in reasonable anticipation of, or for use in, a civil, criminal, or administrative action or proceeding;

NOTE: To support audit readiness it is a wise idea to bookmark the web-site pages of HHS that are pertinent. Printing copies of the web-pages and placing such artifacts in the ARF is a smart way to demonstrate active consultation with HHS guidance.

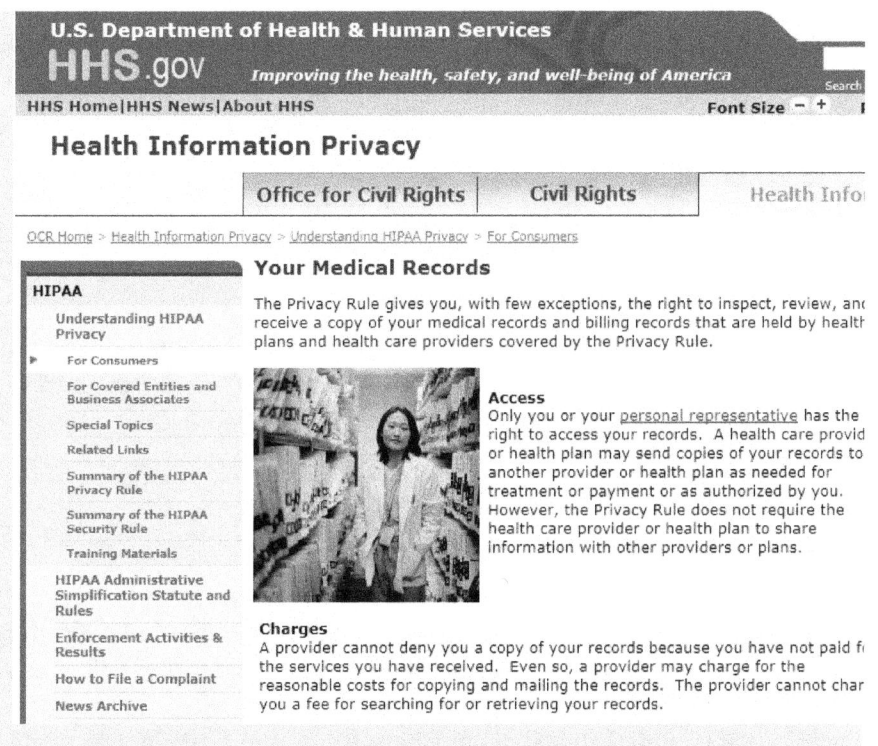

http://www.hhs.gov/ocr/privacy/hipaa/understanding/consumers/medicalrecords.html

DENYING ACCESS

Denying access to medical information concerning an individual is problematic from the start. HIPAA practitioners should keep in mind that without a structured and deliberative process (in writing), decisions to deny access to medical information can appear arbitrary and capricious. Patients that feel their requests for access to records were trivialized, or that they were treated unfairly, have the option to file a complaint with HHS OCR.

Sample HHS OCR audit questions:

§ 164.524(d)(2)	If access to medical information is denied, is there a policy for providing a written denial

§ 164.524(a)	Has the organization documented and implemented a process for denying patient access to or copies of their records?

SUMMARY

This chapter provided a very brief overview how to address the issue of policies and procedures (P&Ps). Examples of areas requiring P&Ps were in the patient access to medical information area. It was noted that it would be wise of the HIPAA novice to review the materials on the HHS OCR web-site[36] to develop a further understanding of policy drivers.

---

[36] http://www.hhs.gov/ocr/privacy/hipaa/understanding/

Dress Code Enforced

In order to provide a safer facility and a family environment, a dress code is strictly enforced.

Excluded Attire:

Clothing that displays offensive matter contrary to the family environment.
Offensive or gang related tattoos openly displayed.
Known validated gang symbols or writing openly displayed or flashed to anyone.
Clothing exposing excessive portions of the skin.
Accessories that appear to be weapons, even if non-operational.
Other non-traditional clothing that is construed to be inappropriate for a family environment.

No clothing or other items will be checked or stored by event staff. You may surrender it to staff for destruction or return the items, if lawful to possess, back to your car. Failure to comply with the dress code or other rules will result in ejection from the event and fairgrounds property.

VIII. ADDRESSABLE VS. REQUIRED

Complying with the HIPAA Privacy and Security Rules by creating the appropriate audit-ready evidence in the form of P&Ps is a formidable task.. If the institution has not completed a comprehensive set of P&Ps staff might want to consider a divide and conquer approach to this task. One strategy would be to create two (2) P&P information buckets: **REQUIRED** and **ADDRESSABLE P&Ps.**

There are some policies that the HHS OCR will consider an absolute must -- these are known as **Required** policies. In contrast, there are some policies that HHS use more flexible on inspection criteria, these are known as **Addressable** policies.

As the reader skims the HIPAA regulations notice some sections are followed by (**Required**) or (**Addressable**).

For instance:

§ 164.308 Administrative safeguards.(a)(1)(ii)

(C) *Sanction policy __(Required).__* Apply appropriate sanctions against workforce members who fail to comply with the security policies and procedures of the covered entity.

§ 164.308 Administrative safeguards.(a)(3)(ii)

(C) *Termination procedures __(Addressable).__* Implement procedures for terminating access to electronic protected health information when the employment of a workforce member ends or as required by determinations made as specified in paragraph (a)(3)(ii)(B) of this section.

Addressable simply means that the institution has some flexibility to "address" the requirement. Addressable does not mean an organization can simply ignore the requirement, rather it means that it can uniquely address the requirement in the context of that organization's particular environment.

HIPAA was not designed to bankrupt an institution by requiring adherence to every regulation and/or standard in a mindless manner. The Addressable option allows an institution to justify a certain practice while relying on the over-arching guidance provided by the specific HIPAA rule.

So, although the Addressable option does give the institution a "way out", the reader should not see this as a free pass. It will still be necessary to perform a risk analysis (much like the data breach notification risk analysis) to address the concerns of the original HIPAA requirement. The organization's risk analysis of an Addressable requirement may address special circumstances where other "compensating controls" are in-place that reduce the need for the HIPAA stated requirement.

NOTE: A compensating control is another control that is in-place that reduces the specific risk in the area under review. For instance, consider a jewelry store. The store is very well lit, there are several closed circuit television (CCTV) in place, diamonds are placed underneath a locked glass case, a police station is only two blocks away, etc., etc. Each one of these security measures is a form of a compensating control to deter and prevent the theft of diamonds.

In HIPAA parlance, imagine the original requirement was "all diamonds must be protected at all times by being locked in a safe (addressable)." The risk analysis would call attention to all of the other compensating controls that have reduced the addressable risk (discussed in more detail later).

Therefore, if the risk assessment indicates that the risk of PHI compromise has been greatly reduced or "compensated" by another control (CCTV cameras) it would be appropriate to articulate this in a risk statement for an Addressable control requirement (specifics discussed in a later chapter).

PROCEDURES: POLICIES DOWNSTREAM

After a series of catastrophic fires, fire chiefs found themselves being personally sued over the implementation of policies at the fire ground during the fighting of a particular fire. Plaintiff's attorneys would often introduce the entire set of fire department policies into a trial as evidence. As the trial progressed each action of the fire chief would be scrutinized against the departmental policy. In many cases, actions were not consistent with the departmental policies. Recall the kitchen sink and "thou shalt" policy discussion.

Policies (design evidence) should provide over-arching guidelines for staff and line managers. Policies should be an embodiment of the institution's commitment to embracing best industry practices and national standards to effectively guide the organization (they should offer flexibility).

Procedures provide for the downstream implementation of policies. Procedures afford the operational staff a consistent checklist or job-aid to fulfill their duties and responsibilities on a routine or periodic basis (operational evidence).

The key here is that the HIPAA requirement has not been ignored by the organization; but, addressed in a way that may not have been specifically spelled out by regulation (see encryption for example).

NOTE: The reader should be careful not to micro-manage the development of such procedures. The core concept here is that supervisors and managers closest to the daily operation of the institution may have better knowledge than a Privacy Officer regarding the tactical implementation and daily decisions made to act in a manner consistent with the HIPAA rules. However, quality gate metrics should have been chosen that create operational evidence when such decisions are made.

As an example. The implementation specifications for the HIPAA Security Rule standard for Security awareness and training include four addressable categories:

§164.308(a) (5)

(i) Standard: Security awareness and training.
Implement a security awareness and training program for all members of its workforce (including management).

(ii) Implementation specifications. Implement:

(A) Security reminders (Addressable). Periodic security updates.

(B) Protection from malicious software (Addressable). Procedures for guarding against, detecting, and reporting malicious software.

(C) Log-in monitoring (Addressable). Procedures for monitoring log-in attempts and reporting discrepancies.

(D) Password management (Addressable). Procedures for creating, changing, and safeguarding passwords.

The above citation offers a clear example of the interplay between policies and procedures. One could make the argument that the over-arching standard for security awareness is embodied in requirement (i) (see above); while the technical implementation details are embodied in (ii) (representing procedures). The Addressable nature of (ii) also illustrates the flexibility that should be afforded to a procedure.

To implement the over-arching requirement for the development of security awareness the institution "addresses" how, for instance, it shall distribute "Security Reminders" (see (ii)(A)).

The institution may address this in a memorandum that speaks to leveraging posters in break-rooms, reminders at staff meetings and "all hands" e-mail alerts.

Repeating the process, an evaluation memorandum might address "Protection from malicious software" ((ii)(B)) by outlining procedures for deploying reminders as to the threat of phishing attacks and spam e-mails sent to the staff. The deployment of an anti-spam e-mail filter might also be utilized. Anti-virus software may be deployed on staff desktop computers to detect virus code, Trojans, worms, malware, adware and the like. Flexibility is afforded the organization to customize the implementation of the policy in a manner that best suits the organization. The memorandum should evaluate the various options weighed and the risks mitigated.

In sum, these procedures are designed to make users aware that unsuccessful log-in attempts are recorded (as they may be an indicator of improper attempts to gain system access).

SUMMARY

This chapter provided a review of the addressable and required policies mandated by the implementing agency regulations of the HHS. It provided examples of addressing policy requirements that allow for flexibility in implementation (addressable polices).

RISK

Dave Sweigert

IX. RISK FRAMEWORK

As one travels amongst the shipping and naval fleets of the world one would most likely observe some similarities. No matter if it is a military or merchant marine ship, an ocean going ship will most likely have a RADAR set and a RADAR operator. The RADAR operator might stand a watch while the ship is underway or if the ship encounters fog. The RADAR operator may have a position on the bridge of the ship, or have some way to immediately contact the bridge (command and control) if a threat to the ship is spotted on the RADAR scope.

As one can see in the RADAR example, protocols and management structure exist to accept the notifications of the RADAR operator. The Captain of the ship doesn't argue the theories of RADAR with the operator. The cook doesn't chime in with his/her view of RADAR operations. The Harbor Master doesn't provide his/her input into the importance of RADAR, etc. The command and control structure of the ship's navigation component has made allowances for the importance of understanding the ship's position and relationship with other ship traffic. In essence, a RADAR management structure or framework has been created that relies on standardized protocols to communicate information.

Without an organizational framework to support the HIPAA compliance efforts one may soon find themselves as the tolerated -- and ignored -- censor in a 1950's television variety show. The creative staff of the variety show begrudgingly tolerate the guy/gal in the corner who is the "censor". But, the impression is that the censor is obviously a social outcast who enjoys stomping on the enjoyment of others and carries an inventory of red flags to throw at people to halt their work efforts.

The "HIPAA" person can be viewed as the "black hat" kill joy that wants to bankrupt the organization with implementation of their lame rules and regulations that they are always pushing on the workforce. In fact, industry periodicals even publish articles announcing that "compliance" is more or less a waste of time and it doesn't provide any real benefits. Information Technology (I.T.) security buffs will openly challenge compliance activities as not as important as "security" activities, etc.

In this environment, it may be prudent for the HIPAA practitioner to portray themselves more as a coach and/or adviser to the organization, rather than the HIPAA enforcer. In a hostile environment it will be important to attempt to construct a quasi-voluntarily cooperative framework that supports HIPAA compliance activities.

It would be hard to imagine a sea-going Captain announcing, "I believe we are in compliance with navigation standards -- after all, we do have a RADAR set." Unfortunately, the RADAR antenna is broken and there is no qualified RADAR operator on board. Imagine the new radio officer points this out to the Captain.

"Well, we have successfully used the RADAR on many occasions in the past when we sailed between Liverpool and Norfolk," the Captain states. But, that was four (4) years ago and the ship now sails between New Orleans and the Azores.

Suffice to say, HIPAA compliance is not a one shot, one time, one person affair. HIPAA compliance programs require maintenance and a path to continuous improvement. As conditions change in the environment (new computer systems, changes in the exterior perimeter of the facility) the HIPAA compliance framework should provide the structure to manage changes to P&Ps, etc.. As the organization's operations become more complex the HIPAA compliance program may need to address these new complexities. The framework will aid in the management of these activities.

An operational framework is an organizational tool that provides for the management of these changes.

X. NIST RISK APPROACH

Sooner or later the topic of NIST will come up. The reader may hear self-proclaimed HIPAA experts use the terms NIST and HIPAA interchangeably. Some organizations will announce that they are "NIST compliant" or "follow NIST and HIPAA standards". Other abuses occur within the profiles of LinkedIn members that list skills, such as: NIST/HIPAA compliance.

NIST stands for the U.S. National Institute for Standards and Technology, a division of the U.S. Department of Commerce. In a manner of speaking, NIST is the federal government's final authority on all things of a technical nature. From fire prevention, to materials handling to microscopes, NIST probably has a standard addressing the issue. When one thinks of NIST they should think of the Good Housekeeping Seal or the Underwriters Laboratories (U.L.).

**National Institute of
Standards and Technology**
U.S. Department of Commerce

Several decades ago, when the computer was an emerging gadget, the computer industry seemed to create standards on the fly. One vendor would build to one standard, another vendor to yet another standard. This frustrated the consistency of systems working together for the federal government, so they began insisting on standards.

In this environment NIST standards became rather important. NIST would create standards for networking components and protocols. Federal laws were then passed mandating the inclusion of NIST standards into federal purchasing contracts. Because NIST standards were embedded in federal purchasing contracts for I.T. equipment a system that did not meet the NIST federal standard was unacceptable to the government (arguably the largest customer of computer and networking products in the world).

This NIST scheme worked so well that soon federal standards were applied to the processes of the I.T. industry. This promoted consistency and standardization amongst federal departments that were purchasing I.T. equipment and services.

Campus of NIST near Rockville, Maryland

Federal laws were passed that required the use of NIST standards for processes and organizational practices to be mandated for all federal agencies[37].

To complicate matters for HIPAA practitioners, the HHS is also a federal agency and must comply with NIST standards in their internal I.T. operations. So, it wasn't much of a leap of faith for HHS OCR to recommend NIST standards as supplemental guidance for entities operating under the HIPAA umbrella. While NIST standards provide valuable insight and standardization of I.T. operations, there is no real requirement for a non-federal government institution to follow the standards of NIST.

Caveat: there is a burgeoning trend for State governments to embrace NIST standards and require their use for I.T. operations. The State of California's Chief Information Security Officer (CISO) (a position appointed by the Governor) has mandated the use of NIST security controls[38] (discussed later).

NIST issues a series of information standards known as Special Publications, or SPs. These publications are considered by many as the gold standard upon which to guide the construction and operation of to build I.T. systems. However, a cautionary note: it can become very expensive to totally embrace the requirements of a NIST SP. Understanding the material presented in a relevant NIST SP is certainly worthwhile; but, the practitioner's job will be to fashion an appropriate mix of NIST SP "guidance" tailored to the organization's technical policies and process requirements.

---

[37] The Computer Security Act of 1987 assigned NIST the responsibility for the development and promulgation of cost-effective computer security standards and guidelines for the federal unclassified systems community.
[38] "NIST Special Publication (SP) 800-53 is set as minimum for information security control requirements for State of California agencies.

Dave Sweigert

NIST'S RISK ASSESSMENT GUIDANCE

This discussion serves as a prelude to the crafting of an organization's risk management framework (RMF), which can be an extension of the HIPAA quality circle or compliance committee. Think of an institution's RMF as a standards based approach to quantify risk.

NIST has several standards that address the formation of a RMF approach. Keep in mind that these standards are valuable reference points; but, are not usually mandatory for a non-governmental organization to embrace. But, HHS OCR has cited several NIST standards as appropriate guidance, especially in the area of risk management ("wink", "wink").

The seminal document in this area is NIST SP 800-30, entitled, *"Risk Management Guide for Information Technology System"*. A copy can be obtained free of charge at the NIST web-site[39]. A Google search of the title should provide the reader with the direct link to an Adobe PDF document.

NIST

National Institute of
Standards and Technology
Technology Administration
U.S. Department of Commerce

Special Publication 800-30

Risk Management Guide for Information Technology Systems

Recommendations of the National Institute of Standards and Technology

Example of NIST publication

---

[39] http://csrc.nist.gov/

SURVING A HIPAA AUDIT

The HIPAA practitioner should pay particular attention to the process flow diagrams and be familiar with these processes to satisfy the HIPAA requirement to assess risk.

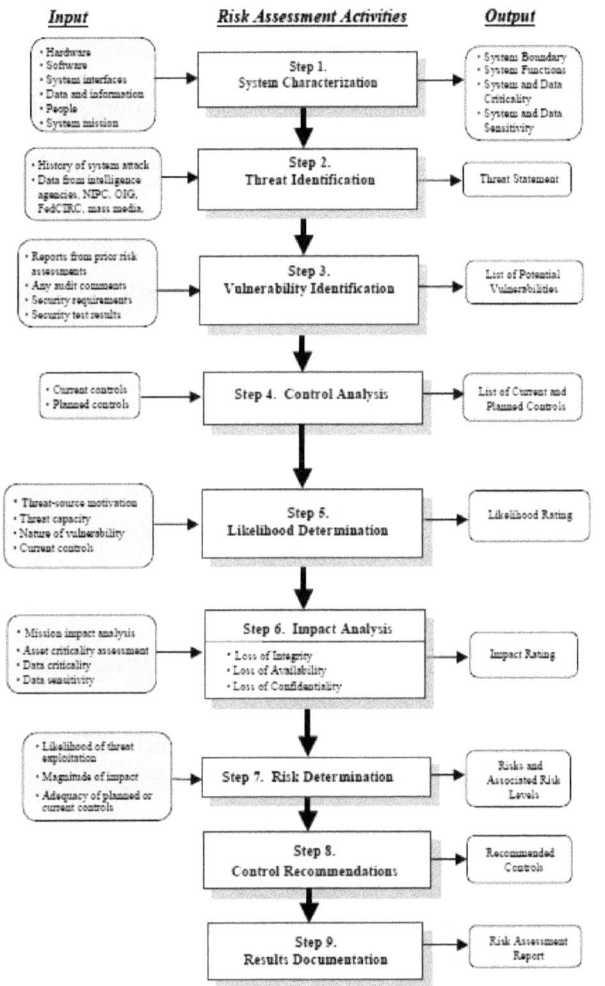

Figure 3-1. Risk Assessment Methodology Flowchart

NIST Risk Management Framework approach

95

NOTE: § 164.308(a)(1)(ii)(A) *Risk analysis* **(Required).**
Conduct an accurate and thorough assessment of the potential risks and vulnerabilities to the confidentiality, integrity, and availability of electronic protected health information held by the covered entity.

This establishes a requirement to conduct a risk analysis of threats and vulnerabilities to the C.I.A. to P.H.I. (discussed in the following chapter).

Sample HHS OCR audit questions:

§ 164.308(a)(1)(ii)(A)	Has the organization developed Risk Assessment and/or Risk Management policies and procedures?

§ 164.308(a)(1)(ii)(A)	Has the organization defined the **frequency** of risk assessments by policy and/or procedures, is there documentation of this?

§ 164.308(a)(1)(ii)(A)	Has the organization identified key operational risks that could result in a breach of ePHI security?

In sum, the purpose of such a risk analysis is to help management prioritize the allocation of strategies and resources to reduce the likelihood of negative consequences. In this context, negative consequences can be impacts to the confidentiality, integrity and availability (C.I.A.) of ePHI.

NOTE: § 164.306 Security standards: General rules.
> **(a) *General requirements.*** Covered entities must do the following:
> **(1)** Ensure the **confidentiality, integrity, and availability** of all **electronic protected health information** the covered entity creates, receives, maintains, or transmits.
> **(2)** Protect against any **reasonably anticipated threats or hazards** to the security or integrity of such information.
> **(3)** Protect against any reasonably anticipated uses or disclosures of such information that are not permitted or required under subpart E of this part.
> **(4)** Ensure compliance with this subpart by its workforce.

The above cite serves as an appropriate introduction to the concept of safeguard, security controls and security measures.

NIST ADVICE ON SECURITY CONTROLS

 Once risks are identified certain actions need to be taken to reduce the likelihood of the risk occurrence or to reduce the severity of the consequences of the risk occurrence.

Recall the HIPAA Security Rule creates three categories to protect P.I.I./P.H.I.: TECHNICAL, ADMINISTRATIVE and PHYSICAL SAFEGUARDS. In this context a safeguard is a control, as in the HIPAA context a "security measure".

NOTE: § 164.306 Security standards: General rules.

> **(b)** *Flexibility of approach.*
>
> **(1)** Covered entities may use **any security measures** that allow the covered entity to **reasonably and appropriately implement** the standards and implementation specifications as specified in this subpart.
>
> **(2)** In deciding which **security measures** to use, a covered entity must take into account the following factors:
>
> **(i)** The size, complexity, and capabilities of the covered entity.
>
> **(ii)** The covered entity's technical infrastructure, hardware, and software security capabilities.
>
> **(iii)** The costs of **security measures.**
>
> **(iv)** The probability and criticality of potential risks to electronic protected health information.

It will help the organization demonstrate compliance to external auditors if standardized language has been used to describe the use of such security controls and safeguards. For this reason, it is helpful to be familiar with NIST SP 800-53, (revision 4), *"Security and Privacy Controls for Federal Information Systems and Organizations."* As with NIST SP 800-30 it is advisable for the HIPAA practitioner to be familiar with key charts that address a RMF approach.

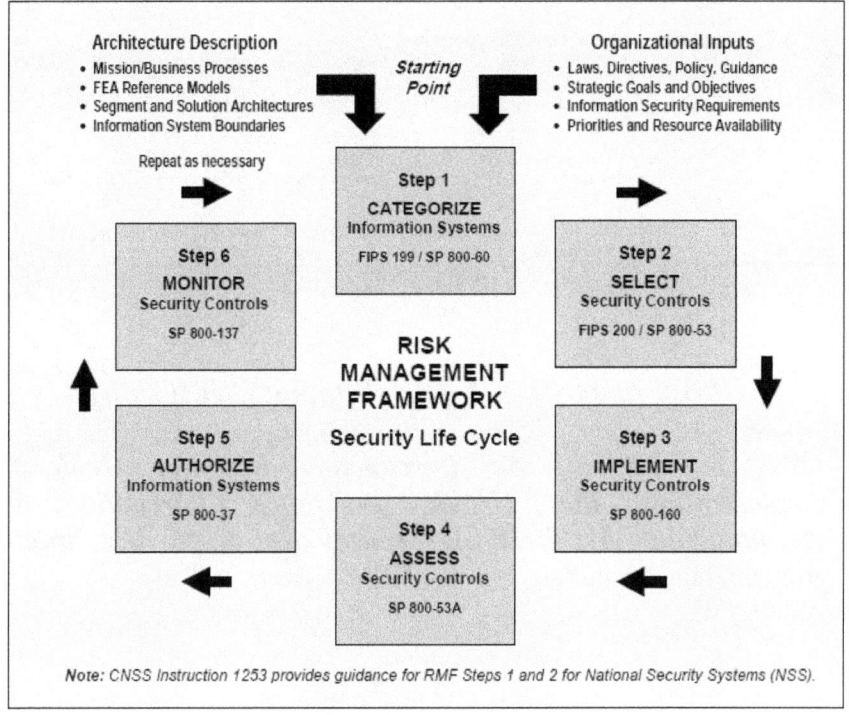

FIGURE 2: RISK MANAGEMENT FRAMEWORK

NIST SP 800-53 (rev 4)

As pictured above, NIST SP 800-53 (rev 4) describes the full life cycle of a RMF. From the initial identification of threats and vulnerabilities, through the re-assessment of the effectiveness of security controls used to address those threats.

NIST SP 800-53 (rev 4) also provides several examples of security controls, grouped by control families. As illustrated below, the very process of creating a Risk Assessment policy is a security control.

FAMILY: RISK ASSESSMENT

RA-1   **RISK ASSESSMENT POLICY AND PROCEDURES**

Control: The organization:

a.   Develops, documents, and disseminates to [*Assignment: organization-defined personnel or roles*]:

   1.   A risk assessment policy that addresses purpose, scope, roles, responsibilities, management commitment, coordination among organizational entities, and compliance; and

   2.   Procedures to facilitate the implementation of the risk assessment policy and associated risk assessment controls; and

NIST 800-53 (rev)

NIST GUIDANCE ON THE HIPAA SECURITY RULE

NIST SP 800-66, *"An Introductory Resource Guide for Implementing the Health Insurance Portability and Accountability Act (HIPAA) Security Rule"*, provides specific implementation guidance on the HIPAA Security Rule.

NIST Special Publication 800-66 Revision 1

NIST
National Institute of
Standards and Technology
U.S. Department of Commerce

An Introductory Resource Guide for Implementing the Health Insurance Portability and Accountability Act (HIPAA) Security Rule

Matthew Scholl, Kevin Stine,
Joan Hash, Pauline Bowen, Arnold Johnson,
Carla Dancy Smith, and Daniel I. Steinberg

I N F O R M A T I O N   S E C U R I T Y

NIST SP 800-66

The HIPAA practitioner will find NIST SP 800-66 especially helpful as it provides several tables that clearly outline the requirements of the HIPAA Security Rule. The example below highlights the requirement to conduct a bona fide risk assessment.

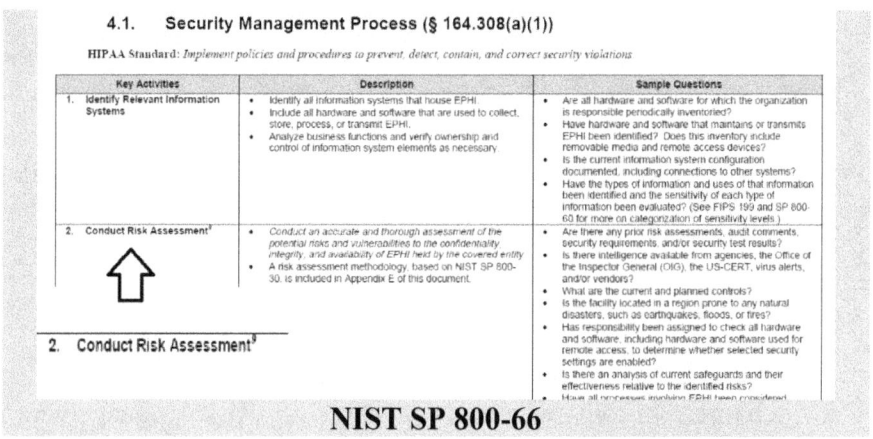

NIST SP 800-66

OTHER SOURCES OF NIST GUIDANCE

- **NIST Special Publication 800-18 (Security Planning)**
- **NIST Special Publication 800-30 (Risk Assessment)**
- **NIST Special Publication 800-39 (Risk Management)**
- **NIST Special Publication 800-53 (Security Controls [SC])**
- **NIST Special Publication 800-53A ([SC] Assessment)**
- **NIST Special Publication 800-60 (Security Category Mapping**

SUMMARY

This chapter introduced the concepts of Risk Management Frameworks (RMF) and touched on guidance offered in NIST publications. It explained the role of NIST as the leading standards body offering publications to provide guidance to privacy practitioners when addressing controls and safeguards.

XI.   THREATS & IMPACTS

The quantification and/or qualification of risks to an organization begins with assessing threats, vulnerabilities and their impact on business assets.

The objective is selecting   realistic cost-effective security safeguards or implementing other types of controls to protect the enterprise.   It can be very wasteful to deploy security controls where they will be ineffective in addressing the threat or closing the vulnerability.

Many entities – especially in the I.T. realm – can be gadget and device driven. The I.T. industry is often driven by the latest virus, worm or Trojan horse panic that proceeds a knee-jerk acquisition of new security software, devices or gadgets.   This can be a wasteful practice, and if poorly documented brings no value to the compliance program.

The proper assessment of risks and the creation of a risk management program is tricky business. For this reason, it will be instructive for the reader to first address the assessment of threats and impacts to business operations.

Sample audit question:

§ 164.308 (a)(1)(ii)(A)	Has the entity identified risks or threats to the facilities or channels that transmit ePHI?

BACKGROUND ON THREAT ASSESSMENT CONCEPT

The threat assessment is part of the ADMINISTRATIVE SAFEGUARD category of the Security Rule. The threat assessment is a building block of the Risk Assessment process.

The threat assessment and business impact analysis can be viewed as a foundational and preliminary activities to prepare the organization prior to engaging in a more complex risk assessment.

There are many methodologies and strategies to assess threats. For the purposes of illustration, fundamental concepts have been borrowed by the U.S. Department of Homeland Security (DHS) to illustrate the process.

NOTE: Before proceeding to far with threat assessment activiries, the reader should ascertain the status of a risk assessment policy and procedure. The activity of producing the threat assessment is operational evidence that will support a risk assessment policy.

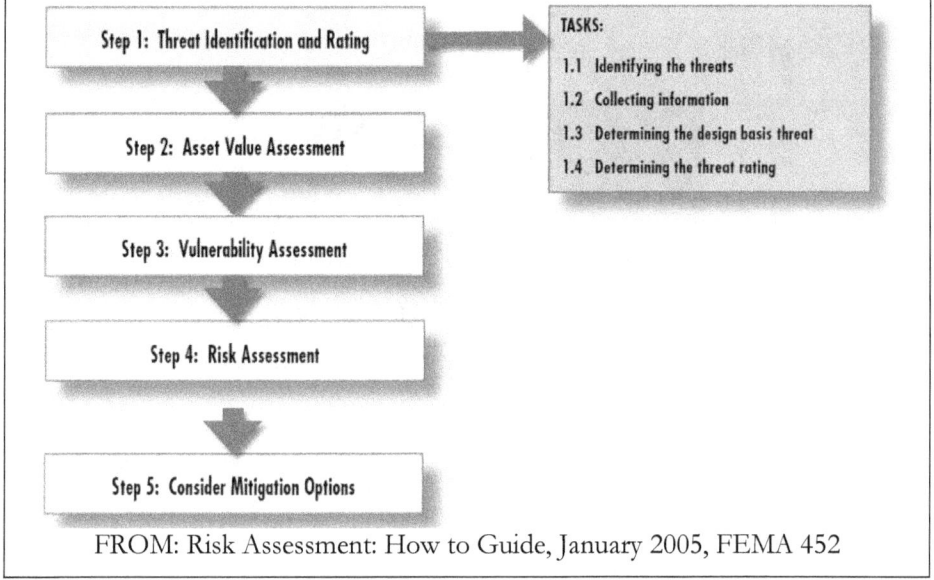

FROM: Risk Assessment: How to Guide, January 2005, FEMA 452

IDENTIFY THREATS & HAZARDS

Threat Identification & Rating

- Identify the threats
- Collecting information
- Determining design basis of the threat (unaddressed herein)
- Determining the threat rating (unaddressed herein)[40]

Identify the Threats and Hazards of Concern. Based on a combination of experience, forecasting, subject matter expertise, and other available resources, identify a list of the threats and hazards of primary concern to the organization[41].

---

[40] Much of the terminology and methodology of the FEMA 452 Handbook is focused on the prevention of terrorism. Some steps will be unaddressed in this booklet as the intent is to use such content for illustrative purposes.

[41] Adopted from U.S. Department of Homeland Security, Risk Lexicon, June 2013

EXAMPLE:

VULNERABILITIES	• Car unlocked • Parked on dark street • No street light • Few police patrols
THREATS	• Gang activity reported in area • Drunk drivers leaving nearby bar

In the above example, the threat agents are active forces that COULD exploit the vulnerabilities of the car. Threats have the capability – but, not necessarily the intent – to cause damage.

Threats impact business assets

Key stakeholder facilitated workshop – or guided discussion – is a great way to engage team members in the threat assessment process. Brainstorming potential threats from a multi-disciplinary team will yield a broad cross section of potential threats.

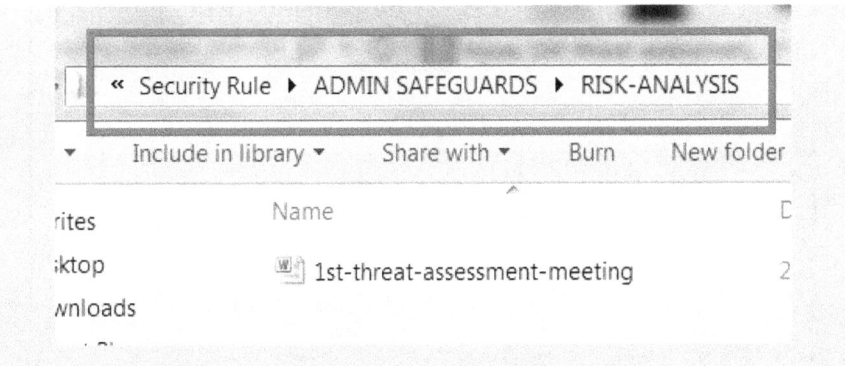

NOTE: Evidence artifacts related to developing the risk assessment should be placed in the ARF.

Agenda	**HIPAA Compliance Team** Monday, March xx, 2015 11:00 AM to 12:00 AM Conference Room

Type of meeting:
Threat
Assessment
Meeting
Facilitator: Barb

Attendees: CFO,
I.T. Manager,
General Counsel,
Privacy Officer,
Optional:

Agenda topics

✓ **Threat Assessment brainstorming**

✓ **Business impact analysis review**

✓ **Building asset inventory**

NOTE: It is important to record the activities associated with threat assessment to demonstrate that reasonable care was applied to the protection of medical information, e-PHI, etc. Above is an example of an agenda announcement for the threat assessment meeting.

PLACE THREATS IN CONTEXT TO IMPACTS

THREAT:
Definition: natural or man-made occurrence, individual, entity, or action that has or indicates the potential to harm life, information, operations, the environment and/or property[42]

ACTIVITY: Place Threats and Hazards within a Context.
ACTIVITY: Place Threats and Hazards within a Context. Develop threat and hazard context descriptions, what should the organization take into account ; such as, the **time**, **date**, and **conditions** in which threats or hazards might occur. Use expert judgment or analysis of probability and statistics to refine descriptions of the different threat and hazard conditions.

Threat/Hazard	Power failure	Hacker attack
Context Description	Worst opportunity for power failure on 29th of month when monthly invoices are being prepared, occurring during normal business hours.	Worst case identity thieves break into enterprise and steal complete medical records or launch ransomware attack to infect all desktops.

This approach describes a situational or circumstances in which the threat has exploited a vulnerability (weakness).

---

[42] Page 33, DHS Risk Lexicon, September 2008

ASSEST VALUATION

Assign a Value to Assets. Evaluate costs associated with the loss of key assets. This can include **people:** (workforce members) clients/customers; **property:** (tangible and intangible) information systems, networking components, reputation; **information**: customer lists, P.H.I., P.I.I., etc.

One approach is to develop an asset inventory. Again a facilitated brainstorming workshop may help with this. The Chief Financial Officer or I.T. Operations Manager might also have inventories in list form.

Asset Valuation		
People	**Things**	**Information**
150 workforce members	$ 2 Million Data Center	8 Million PHI records

In the vulnerable car example, assume the value of the car be $10,000.00. However, there may be a $10,000 computer system in the trunk. The computer may contain intellectual property valued at $250,000. The reader can see that including hidden values in a total is important. Therefore, the asset register or asset inventory should identify the asset and the totality of its worth.

Asset Valuation	
Automobile	$10,000
Computer	$10,000
Intellectual Property	$250,000

TOTAL BUSINESS IMPACT

A threat can impact an asset, if it exploits the asset's vulnerability. But, what is the measurable impact to business operations once a threat impacts an asset?

Business impact measures the totality of the loss on business operations if the business asset is lost. In the automobile example, assume delivery of the $10,000 computer with the $250,000 worth of intellectual property (I.P.) was going to be delivered to a customer in the morning for an agreed upon price of $500,000? Now the loss and total impact on business operations is approaching $770,000 (car + computer + I.P. + delivery).

There are several methods to account and quantify such estimates. It is advisable that you involve the organization C.F.O. who may be considering business insurance for such negative circumstances.

Impacts to systems can also be classified as HIGH, MEDIUM or LOW, as discussed in NIST SP 800-30.

Table 3-5. Magnitude of Impact Definitions

	Impact Definition
High	Exercise of the vulnerability (1) may result in the highly costly loss of major tangible assets or resources; (2) may significantly violate, harm, or impede an organization's mission, reputation, or interest; or (3) may result in human death or serious injury.
Medium	Exercise of the vulnerability (1) may result in the costly loss of tangible assets or resources; (2) may violate, harm, or impede an organization's mission, reputation, or interest; or (3) may result in human injury.
Low	Exercise of the vulnerability (1) may result in the loss of some tangible assets or resources or (2) may noticeably affect an organization's mission, reputation, or interest.

NIST SP 800-66

RISK DASHBOARD

After completing the previously described activities to assess threats, vulnerabilities and impacts to assets, the privacy practitioner can begin to build a risk dash-board.

Risk is essentially a function of the estimated loss caused by a threat agent and the probability such a threat exploits a vulnerability.

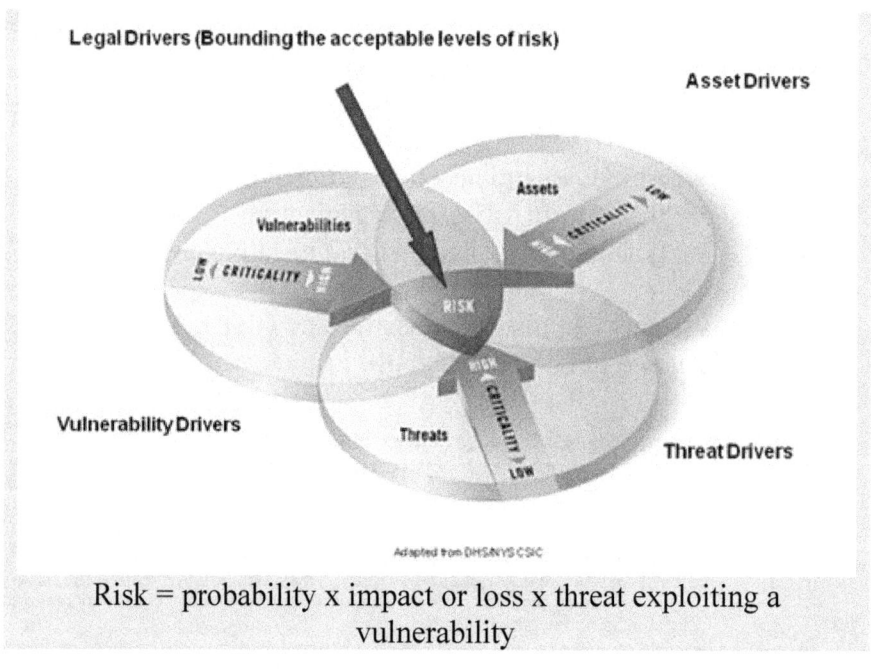

Risk = probability x impact or loss x threat exploiting a vulnerability

Risks can be assigned a weighted quantitative number to help senior leadership prioritize risks. This prioritization will help in developing a Corrective Action Plan (CAP), discussed later.

PROB-ABILITY	LOW	MEDIUM	HIGH
	LOW	MEDIUM	MEDIUM
	LOW	LOW	LOW
IMPACT ON ASSETS →			

As seen above, a low probability of occurrence with a low impact (loss) might receive a rating of L/L (Probability Low, Impact Low).

On the other hand, a high probability event with a high impact might receive a rating of H/H (Probability High, Impact High).

Such an index can then be used to prioritize risks.

Threat-Vulnerability	Risk Rating
Power Black-out, No UPS	M/H
Civil Unrest, Arson	L/H
Mid-range employee quits	M/L

CAUTION: The previous example is overly simplistic. Calculations and deliberations about risks, vulnerabilities, and threats should be undertaken with advice and consultation from credible experts.

Keep in mind, such deliberative information may be discoverable in the event of legal action or a data breach investigation. Exercise caution to avoid inflating threats and impacts, as staff may have to explain to a jury why the institution took no action to counter a risk that was discussed and documented. Again, the "sky is falling" approach to threat exaggeration will not be viewed as helpful during this process. Be realistic in estimates.

SUMMARY

This chapter provided a summary of the risk assessment process. This process identifies threats and vulnerabilities. The process also identifies downstream consequences to assets if threat agents exploit such vulnerabilities. Business loss was discussed and a risk prioritization scheme that assigned a probability to the risk and its impact.

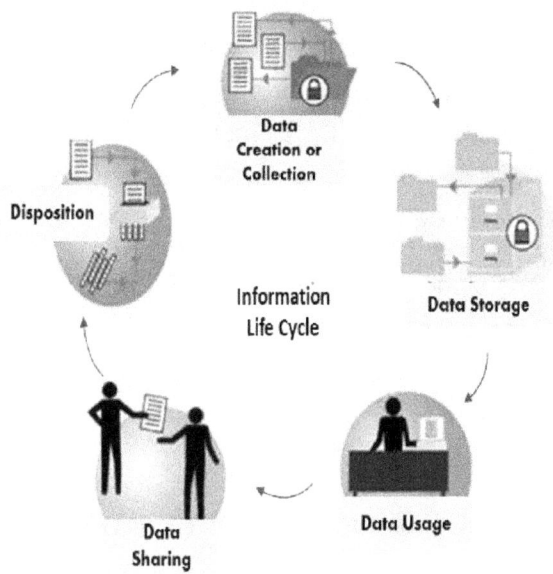

XII. PRIVACY RISK

This chapter leverages the common body of knowledge (CBK) within the privacy advocate community to provide the HIPAA/HITECH practitioner with a wider perspective of privacy issues and to provide more tools in the privacy toolbox.

The reader will find this chapter addressing a more broad subject -- that of privacy terms of art; such as the Fair Information Practice Principles (FIPP), the Privacy Impact Assessment (PIA) and the Data Flow Diagram (DFD). The FIPP, PIA and DFD are not HIPAA specific terms; however, the principles invoked by these terms can be broadly applied to an organization that collects personally identifiable information (PII).

The reader should verify if the institution is subject to the federal Privacy Act of 1974 (Privacy Act) which is applied primarily to federal agencies of the United States that have deployed systems of records that may contain P.I.I. As many states have used the P.A. as a template for localized state law, it is prudent to verify the P.A.'s impact on the organization.

Assuming there is no direct regulatory impacted created by the P.A. on the institution that does not preclude adoption as an industry best practice. The HIPAA practitioner will find striking similarities between the privacy protection provisions of the HIPAA Privacy Rule and the P.A.

FAIR INFORMATION PRACTICE PRINCIPLES

As described on the web-site of the U.S. Department of Homeland Security:[43]

- The FIPPs are a widely accepted framework that is at the core of the Privacy Act of 1974 and is mirrored in the laws of many U.S. states, as well as many foreign nations and international organizations. The concept of defining principles to be used in the evaluation and consideration of systems, processes, or programs that impact individual privacy is not a new one.

- The DHS Privacy Office, therefore, has adopted the FIPPs as its privacy policy framework and seeks to apply them to the full breadth and diversity of DHS programs and activities.

For instructive purposes, below is an example of how the DHS applies the FIPPs to their organization.

---

[43] http://www.dhs.gov/compliance

FAIR INFORMATION PRACTICE PRINCIPLES

- Transparency: DHS should be transparent and provide notice to the individual regarding its collection, use, dissemination, and maintenance of personally identifiable information (PII).

- Individual Participation: DHS should involve the individual in the process of using PII and, to the extent practicable, seek individual consent for the collection, use, dissemination, and maintenance of PII. DHS should also provide mechanisms for appropriate access, correction, and redress regarding DHS's use of PII.

- Purpose Specification: DHS should specifically articulate the authority that permits the collection of PII and specifically articulate the purpose or purposes for which the PII is intended to be used

- Data Minimization: DHS should only collect PII that is directly relevant and necessary to accomplish the specified purpose(s) and only retain PII for as long as is necessary to fulfill the specified purpose(s).

- Use Limitation: DHS should use PII solely for the purpose(s) specified in the notice. Sharing PII outside the Department should be for a purpose compatible with the purpose for which the PII was collected.

- Data Quality and Integrity: DHS should, to the extent practicable, ensure that PII is accurate, relevant, timely, and complete.

- Security: DHS should protect PII (in all media) through appropriate security safeguards against risks such as loss, unauthorized access or use, destruction, modification, or unintended or inappropriate disclosure.

- Accountability and Auditing: DHS should be accountable for complying with these principles, providing training to all employees and contractors who use PII, and auditing the actual use of PII to demonstrate compliance with these principles and all applicable privacy protection requirements.

Source:

http://www.dhs.gov/xlibrary/assets/privacy/privacy_policyguide_2008-01.pdf

Recall the previous patient rights chapter that discussed the patient's right of access to medical records. Many of these rights can be mapped to the FIPPs. For instance:

HIPAA Privacy Rule	FIPPs
Inspect and obtain a copy of all PHI related to individual (§ 164.504(e)(1)) … amend and/or correct PHI (§ 164.504(e)(3)	Data Quality and Integrity Individual Participation
Receive an accounting of the use and disclosures of their PHI .. (§ 164.528)	Transparency
Right to notice (§ 164.520)	Transparency
Full description of the use and processing of PHI (§ 164.520)	Transparency

Although the FIPPs are not a regulatory component of HIPAA – and therefore CEs/BAs are under no obligation to adhere to them – FIPPs can help facilitate a top-down approach to privacy implementation at an organization. It sets the "tone at the top" and represents a set of principles that can be endorsed by a Board of Trustees, senior leadership, executives, etc.

The FIPPs also serve instructive purposes. As an example, according to the HHS internal cyber security office[44], the FIPPs served as the basis for the create of the NIST Privacy Framework, which is codified in Appendix J of the NIST SP 800-53 (rev 4). As described below, the reader could rely on Appendix J to create a privacy risk assessment for the purposes of limiting exposure due to privacy risks.

---

[44]

http://www.hhs.gov/ocio/securityprivacy/awarenesstraining/privac yawarenesstraining.pdf

PRIVACY IMPACT ASSESSMENT

The Privacy Impact Assessment (PIA) is the term the P.A. applies to a privacy risk assessment – although PIAs are created for the purposes of accessing the impact of newly procured federal government I.T. systems.

Federal government agencies are required under Section 208 of the E-Government Act of 2002 (Public Law 107-347, 44 U.S.C. Chapter 36) to conduct a PIA before developing or procuring IT systems, or initiating new information collections that use IT, that collects, maintains or disseminates PII.

The HIPAA practitioner may find it useful to leverage the terminology of the PIA to infuse more clout into the activity of accessing privacy risk. Additionally, by using a term associated with a leading best industry practice (PIA) it establishes a sense of authority with the assessment (this may be useful in the unfortunate event of civil litigation).

NOTE: Although the reader's organization may not be a government agency, there may gain significant gravitas by voluntarily aspiring to the FIPPs/PIA baseline. Especially in cases where the institution may be storing consumer related data -- such as positioning data of customer cell phone locations (see Global Positioning System (GPS)[45]).

Perhaps the greatest benefit of the PIA process will be to identify specific systems, applications or programs that are processing, collecting or transmitting PII/ePHI, etc. This will help the HIPAA practitioner identify discrete, specific systems (collections of servers, networks, disk arrays, desktops, etc.).

---

[45] See Federal Trade Commission report, *Protecting Consumer Privacy in an Era of Rapid Change: Recommendations for Businesses and Policymakers* (Washington, D.C.: March 2012).

Privacy Impact Assessment
for the

Watchlist Service

July 14, 2010

Contact Point
Justin Matthes
Director, Transborder Screening Initiatives
Screening Coordination Office
Office of Policy
Department of Homeland Security

Reviewing Official
Mary Ellen Callahan
Chief Privacy Officer
Department of Homeland Security
(703) 235-0780

Example of a federal government Privacy Impact Assessment

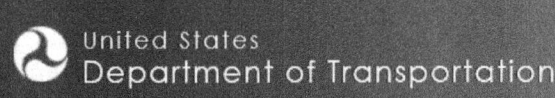

Home > Resources > For Individuals > Privacy

PIA - Identity Management System (IDMS)

DEPARTMENT OF TRANSPORTATION

Federal Aviation Administration

Privacy Impact Assessment
Identity Management System (IDMS) &
Personal Identity Verification Cards (PIV Cards)

http://www.dot.gov/individuals/privacy/pia-identity-management-system-idms

What PIA offers the HIPAA practitioner is the tool to identify stand-alone, discrete systems that process ePHI/PII, in contrast to the development of organization P&Ps that guide activities. The identification of such systems will become increasing important to the downstream activities of producing more and more complex risk assessments to protect ePHI/PII, etc.

In a perfect world, a PIA would be required before a system processing ePHI/PII went into "live" operation. The more the PIA process is embedded into the design phase of a system the better.

Privacy impact assessments (PIAs) are a tool that you can use to identify and reduce the privacy risks of your projects. A PIA can reduce the risks of harm to individuals through the misuse of their personal information. It can also help you to design more efficient and effective processes for handling personal data.

You can integrate the core principles of the PIA process with your existing project and risk management policies. This will reduce the resources necessary to conduct the assessment and spreads awareness of privacy throughout your organisation.

U.K.'s Information Commissioner's Office (ICO) web-site[46].

Conducting privacy impact assessments code of practice

https://ico.org.uk/media/for-organisations/documents/1595/pia-code-of-practice.pdf

---

[46] https://ico.org.uk/for-organisations/guide-to-data-protection/privacy-by-design/

DATA FLOW DIAGRAM

One of the most illustrative artifacts that will be produced by the PIA process will be the Data Flow Diagram (DFD), also referred to as a "data map" or "data mapping". The DFD will provide the practitioner with a high-level view of the components of a particular system.

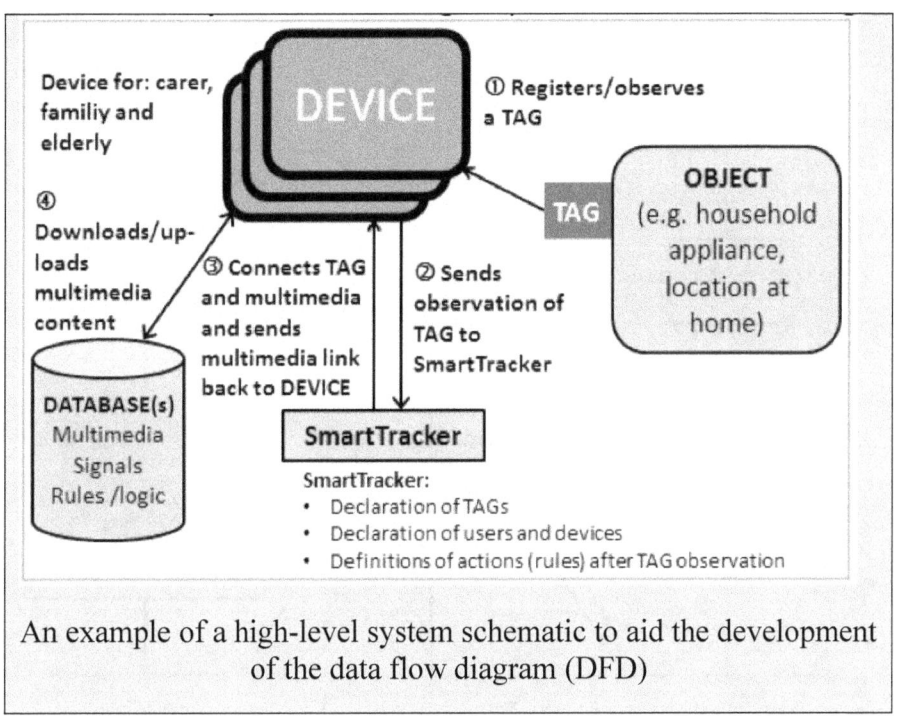

An example of a high-level system schematic to aid the development of the data flow diagram (DFD)

The development of the DFD represents an excellent interfacing opportunity between the HIPAA practitioner and the system owners and/or engineering staff designing/operating the system under assessment. The DFD assessment process is focused towards creating the DFD, which can take place in a facilitated workshop or other interactions. The end goal of the first phase of the DFD development process is to have a complete system schematic.

Pediatric Developmental Screening Flowchart

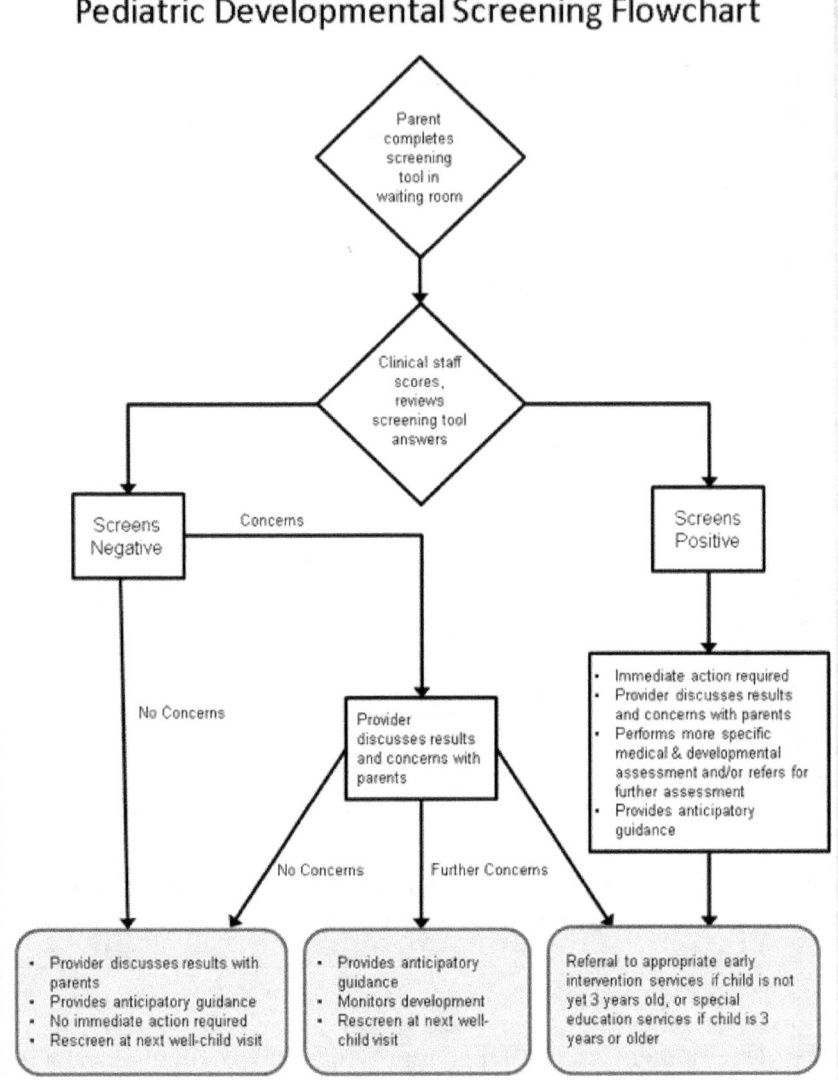

Example of a type of data flow diagram (DFD)

http://www.cdc.gov/ncbddd/childdevelopment/images/screening-chart.gif

During the documentation phase (DFD) it is helpful to follow a model to determine the Data Life Cycle. Mapping the data life cycle to the DFD should provide a comprehensive view of the movement of data within the organization. This creates the data mapping artifact.

Data Life Cycle	
Creation	Initial collection of data (the birth). May constrain the collection of unnecessary data as a protective control. Data intake.
Storage and Transmission	Considerations given to physical storage, tracking, receipt, management within the enterprise. Workstation security.
Use	Data classification issues (sensitive, confidential?). Limited use. How is it used to drive decision-making? Access control issues. User training and awareness issues.
Sharing	Is data shared with third parties? Aggregation of data? Third parties that have access? Business Associate Agreements?
Retention and Destruction	Archived data and legal discovery process. Confirmed destruction of expired data. Shredding, etc. Retention policy?

PRIVACY CONTROL CATALOG

The federal Privacy Control Catalog (PCC) is embodied within Appendix J of the NIST SP 800-53 (rev 4). It specifically addresses systems that contain PII. Again, the use of the PCC maybe a mandatory implementing control for federal agencies that process, receive, transmit and store PII and this may not have direct applicability to some CEs/BAs. However, the practitioner should ensure that this is not the case as the CE/BA may store or process PII related to federal employees as part of federal programs, etc.

Special Publication 800-53 Revision 4   Security and Privacy Controls for Federal Information Systems and Organizations

APPENDIX J

PRIVACY CONTROL CATALOG
PRIVACY CONTROLS, ENHANCEMENTS, AND SUPPLEMENTAL GUIDANCE

The need to protect an individual's privacy is as important today as it was in 1974 when the Privacy Act first sought to balance the government's need to collect information from an individual with a citizen's right to be notified as to how that information was being used, collected, maintained, and disposed of after the requisite period of use. These concerns are also shared in the private sector, where healthcare, financial, and other services continue to be delivered via the web with increasingly higher levels of personalization. The proliferation of social media, Smart Grid, mobile, and cloud computing, as well as the transition from structured to unstructured data and metadata environments, have added significant complexities and challenges for federal organizations in safeguarding privacy. These challenges extend well beyond the traditional information technology security view of protecting privacy which focused primarily on ensuring confidentiality. Now there are greater implications with respect to controlling the integrity of an individual's information, and with ensuring that an individual's information is available on demand. The challenging landscape requires federal organizations to expand their view of privacy, in order to meet citizen expectations of privacy that go beyond information security.

http://nvlpubs.nist.gov/nistpubs/SpecialPublications/NIST.SP.800-53r4.pdf#page=432

The PCC articulates implementing control terminology, a page is used to address each individual control to provide guidance (see below).

ID	PRIVACY CONTROLS
DM-3	Minimization of PII Used in Testing, Training, and Research
IP	**Individual Participation and Redress**
IP-1	Consent
IP-2	Individual Access
IP-3	Redress
IP-4	Complaint Management
SE	**Security**
SE-1	Inventory of Personally Identifiable Information
SE-2	Privacy Incident Response
TR	**Transparency**
TR-1	Privacy Notice
TR-2	System of Records Notices and Privacy Act Statements
TR-3	Dissemination of Privacy Program Information
UL	**Use Limitation**
UL-1	Internal Use
UL-2	Information Sharing with Third Parties

Appendix J – NIST SP 800 -53 (rev 4)

IP-2   INDIVIDUAL ACCESS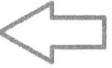

Control: The organization:

a. Provides individuals the ability to have access to their personally identifiable information (PII) maintained in its system(s) of records;

b. Publishes rules and regulations governing how individuals may request access to records maintained in a Privacy Act system of records;

c. Publishes access procedures in System of Records Notices (SORNs); and

d. Adheres to Privacy Act requirements and OMB policies and guidance for the proper processing of Privacy Act requests.

Appendix J – NIST SP 800 -53 (rev 4)

AVOIDING DISJOINTED PRACTICES

The end goal of using the previously discussed tools is to produce artifacts that will bring transparency to the privacy process. PII/ePHI buried in an unknown database will be difficult to identify for a privacy practitioner without the use of some structured tool-sets.

As the DFD or data map begin to take shape it will become easier to identify the flow of data and sensitive information. Privacy policies can then be mapped to the information flow diagram to verify that appropriate policies addresses sensitive data as it flows through the enterprise.

In the end, the top-down endorsement of the FIPPs should drive an appropriate privacy policy that touches upon the secure collection, handling and storage of ePHI/PII. By creating the artifacts discussed – such as the PIA and DFD – the practitioner will be able to facilitate the "bottom-up" development of artifacts, Taken together (PIA and DFD) the practitioner should have visibility as to gaps in policy that need to be addressed.

Using the eight families of controls contained in Appendix J[47] (PCC), the privacy practitioner should be able to identify which controls are used in a system to protected that data (designed to protect PII, but can be used for ePHI as well). This legitimizes the conversations between the privacy practitioner and the I.T. system owners and technical implementers.

In the end, the practitioner needs to measure how well the privacy policy has spread throughout the organization – including the world of the I.T. staff. This is another element of business risk and should be treated as such.

---

[47] Appendix J, *Privacy Control Catalog* to *Security and Privacy Controls for Federal Information Systems and Organizations*, NIST Special Publ. (SP) 800-53, Rev. 4 (April 30, 2013)

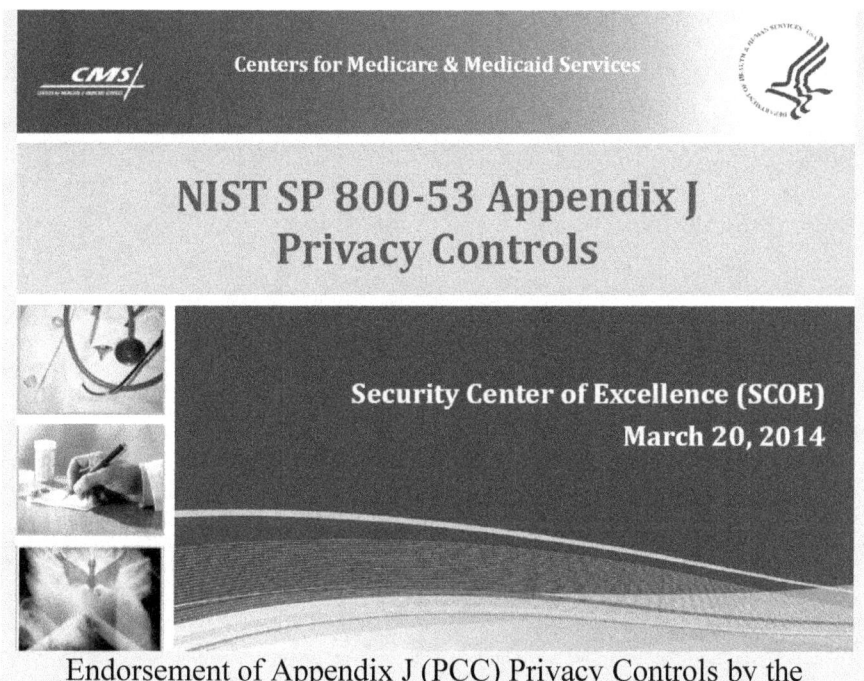

Endorsement of Appendix J (PCC) Privacy Controls by the
Centers for Medicare and Medicaid Services (CMS)

SUMMARY

This chapter introduced the federal Privacy Act of 1974 and terms
of art associated with the privacy community. It explained the
usefulness of a Privacy Impact Assessment (PIA) and Data Flow
Diagram (DFD). These tools can be valuable items in the privacy
practitioner's tool kit and offer leverage to marry privacy controls
with security controls (as outlined in Appendix J of NIST SP 800-
53 (rev 4)).

XIII. PHYSICAL SAFEGUARD THREAT ASSESSMENT

This chapter offers the reader a practical exercise in the threat assessment process. A threat assessment of the building that contains e-PHI/PHI will be undertaken. This will create the following artifact: preliminary threat assessment that addresses the **PHYSICAL SAFEGUARDS** category of the HIPAA Security Rule.

A good check list for this type of activity has been produced by the **Payment Card Industry** (PCI) as part of the **Data Security Standard** (DSS). Although the PCI-DSS is not a HIPAA mandated requirement or standard, it can be very illustrative of potential physical threats to PHI/e-PHI.

NOTE: see *PCI-DSS Requirement 9: Restrict physical access to cardholder data* for more information and a security check-list. This PCI DSS check-list is a mere suggestion, other check-lists are available – use what is appropriate for the situation.

The organization may have a facility security officer (F.S.O.). The F.S.O. may have conducted such threat/vulnerability assessments in the past. The HIPAA practitioner should examine these historical reports. If there is no F.S.O., the HIPAA quality circle should consider developing a plan to have a designated point of contact (P.O.C.) to address physical security concerns.

In the end, the objective of addressing the PHYSICAL SAFEGUARD inspection is to have identified the major threats/vulnerabilities to the physical facility that contains ePHI and PHI. Document the findings and make liberal use of reports that third parties can provide.

For instance, the HIPAA practitioner may desire to have three (3) separate burglar alarm companies provide the institution with quotes for an alarm system. Some police departments also provide such a service. Save these quotes and/or documents in the audit readiness folder (ARF) under an appropriate file name for PHYSICAL SAFEGUARDS.

If there is no documentation in the **ARF**, there is no indication that an organization identified physical vulnerabilities to the facility; which will create doubt for a jury or an investigator. NOTE: it is a requirement to have appropriate P&Ps for the protection of the facility[48].

[48] § 164.310 Physical safeguards.
A covered entity must, in accordance with § 164.306:
(a)
(1) *Standard: Facility access controls.* Implement policies and procedures to limit physical access to its electronic information systems and the facility or facilities in which they are housed, while ensuring that properly authorized access is allowed.

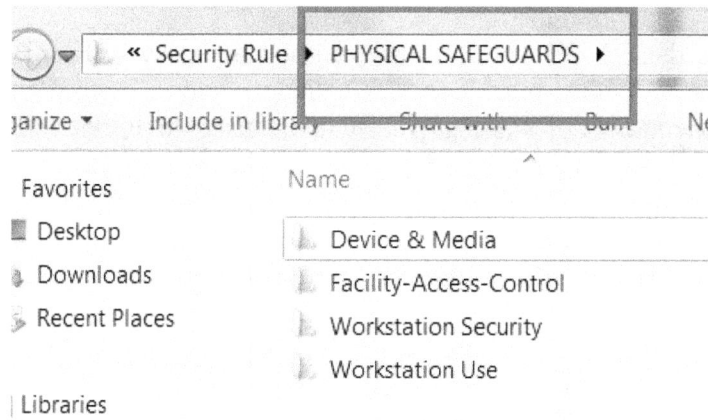

Example of file directory in ARF

NIST Special Publication 800-53 (Rev. 4), "*Security Controls and Assessment Procedures for Federal Information Systems and Organizations*", provides a list of suggested controls, grouped within "control families". This may be a source of guidance when completing the PHYSICAL SAFEGUARDS vulnerability study; for instance:

PE-1 - PHYSICAL AND ENVIRONMENTAL PROTECTION POLICY AND PROCEDURES

PE-2 - PHYSICAL ACCESS AUTHORIZATIONS

PE-3 - PHYSICAL ACCESS CONTROL

PE-4 - ACCESS CONTROL FOR TRANSMISSION MEDIUM,.[49]

---

[49] https://nvd.nist.gov/

Again, these NIST publications are not mandatory standards to be complied with; but, provide guidance to the practitioner. Documentation of findings that can be used in P&Ps following consultation with NIST SP 800-53 would be a prudent activity. Such activity demonstrates that the recommended HHS OCR source of guidance was consulted to develop the PHYSICAL SAFEGUARD vulnerability study.

Example of fire inspection

§164.310(a)(2)(ii)	Does organization have documentation of facility inventory, physical maintenance records, the history of physical changes, upgrades, and other modifications?

§164.310(a)(2)(ii)	Does organization have written procedures that address the physical security of facilities, including the exterior, the interior, and physical plant equipment?

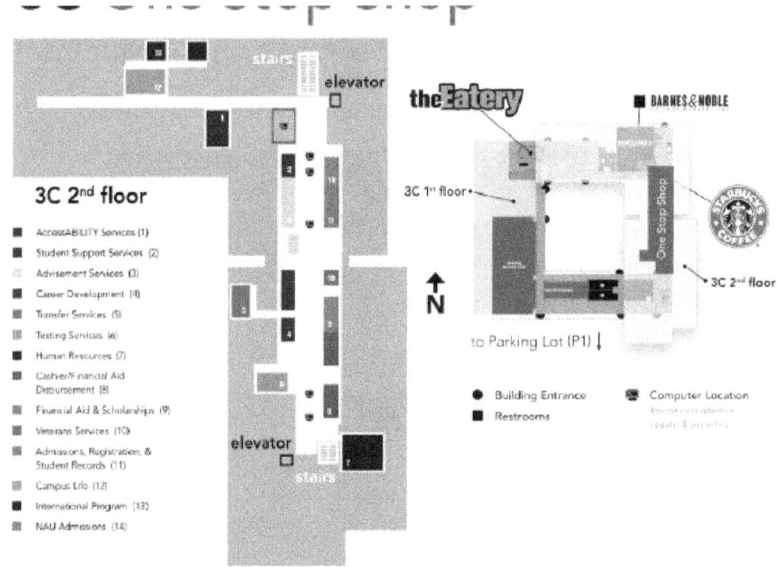

Example of blue-print or floor-plan

§164.310(a)(2)	Does organization have a facility security plan in-place, under revision, or under development?

Examples of physical threats to secure facility

Potential of train derailment on nearby R&R tracks

Fires, garages, chemical storage, paint lockers

Power grid failure

Examples of PHYSICAL SAFEGUARDS

Visitor Control Points

Physical lighting

Security Camera

SUMMARY

This chapter provided guidance on the usefulness of a physical security risk assessment. Tools were presented that could be used as a baseline to measure physical security vulnerabilities.

Cyber Resilience Review and the Framework

Relationship between DHS' Cyber Resilience Review and the NIST Cybersecurity
Framework *[CRR to NIST CSF crosswalk available]*

XIV. ASSESSING COMPLIANCE RISK

Compliance risk describes the risk imposed upon an organization for gaps in the compliance framework; e.g. the lack of current P&Ps. Traditionally, a P&P is considered valid when it is (1) no longer in a draft state, (2) has been formally approved by an authorizing official, (3) and has been dated. The example below would be the accurate description of a policy:

Sanction Policy	Issued 6/6/2014	Signed by B. Sims

When P&Ps are missing, or are outdated, this represents a compliance risk. The impact of a compliance risk may be fines and sanctions imposed on an organization by the HHS OCR. As discussed earlier, the downstream effects of policies are the implementation of procedures. Procedures produce operation evidence of compliance. When no P&Ps exist, or are outdated, then the organization cannot really demonstrate compliance. Thus the compliance risk.

Over the years many organizations may have developed unwritten and informal procedures to conduct business. Sally the records clerk may have always backed-up the day's record notations to a DVD on her desktop around 6 pm. Sally has been doing this for years. The informal and unwritten procedure seems to work just fine.

One of the concerns with this scenario, is that this situation creates a compliance risk. Without a formalized procedure (which is not in draft form, authorized by an official and has an effective date) there really is no way to measure compliance of the data back-up procedure relied upon by the organization.

As P&Ps are a fundamental cornerstone to building a mature compliance program, the lack of P&Ps should be assessed as a vulnerabilities, very similar to the physical security vulnerabilities identified in the previous chapter.

SECURITY BASELINE

The HIPAA practitioner will need to assist the organization in developing a current, robust set of P&Ps that establish the security controls baseline. This may include the development of P&Ps that incorporate best industry practices, parts of NIST standards, HIPAA regulatory references, etc.

P&Ps are used to develop the institution's security governance framework. Security governance is a term that refers to guidance provided to the workforce on how to conduct themselves and their operations to ensure closer compliance with the HIPAA Privacy & Security Rules. This is also known as a security controls baseline or a compliance controls baseline. A baseline will provide a minimum set of P&Ps from which to build and improve upon.

NIST SP 800-100, *"Information Security Handbook: A Guide for Managers,"* can further amplify the construction of a security policy or security controls baseline. Such baseline development can become very technical and it is therefore suggested that the appropriate technical managers participate in this process.

P&P INVENTORY

An inventory of P&Ps should be completed for the purposes of identifying gaps in the compliance policy baseline. The inventory should align with the REQUIRED HIPAA requirements at a minimum; but, it is preferable that there is alignment with ADDRESSABLE requirements as well.

In the case of Addressable, memorandums explaining how the institution will address the particular requirement are still needed – albeit they may not be in the form of a formal policy (see the example of log-in monitoring in previous chapters).

It is important that the risk management framework (RMF) be used to track compliance risk just as any other risk to the organization. The HIPAA committee or quality circle needs to understand that a gap in a Required policy can result in a sanction or fine to the organization. Such a fine is a tangible and measurable impact of negative consequences to the organization.

Compliance risk has been specifically highlighted in this chapter as it has a direct bearing on the preparations for audit readiness. If P&Ps are outdated, or non-existent, this creates a challenge to overcome to achieve audit readiness. In this context compliance risk differs from classical TECHNICAL SAFEGUARD risks and falls into the ADMINISTRATIVE SAFEGUARD risk category.

SUMMARY

This chapter broached the issue of compliance risk. It was explained that compliance risk can be considered a risk to the organization as such vulnerabilities can result in fines and sanctions. Therefore, it was explained, compliance can be treated in the risk management framework as other traditional risks to the organization.

XV. RISKS TO PHI and ePHI

Chances are, the underlying computer systems and network infrastructure have been in place for years. Things have been fine – except for a few "fire drills" here and there. Now, out of the blue, the HIPAA practitioner approaches the I.T. staff with a compliance requirement.

There may be push back from the I.T. technical staff that feel they have already implemented a "pretty good" security program (in their words). Such technical staff members may resent the implication that the deployment of such safeguards in previous years are now being scrutinized for effectiveness.

Meanwhile, the HIPAA practitioner needs to document how these technical safeguards mitigate threats to the organization. The conversation should begin around the threat assessment and move towards clearly identifying risks to PHI and ePHI. Then safeguards should be mapped (traceability) to those risks as mitigation strategies.

As explained in previous chapters, a risk to ePHI and PHI is a risk to the organization, to quote the HHS OCR:

> ".. Risk can be understood as a function of 1) the likelihood of a given threat triggering or exploiting a particular vulnerability, and 2) the resulting impact on the organization. This means that risk is not a single factor or event, but rather it is a combination of factors or events (threats and vulnerabilities) that, if they occur, may have an adverse impact on the organization..."[50]

Over the years the institution may have implemented safeguards on an ad hoc basis as part of good business practices; but, did not map such controls to any particular risk mitigation. In many cases these safeguards are not directly (or even indirectly) traceable to a threat. Therefore, it becomes incumbent upon the HIPAA practitioner to help educate the organization about what risk is, and how safeguards should be mapped to their mitigation.

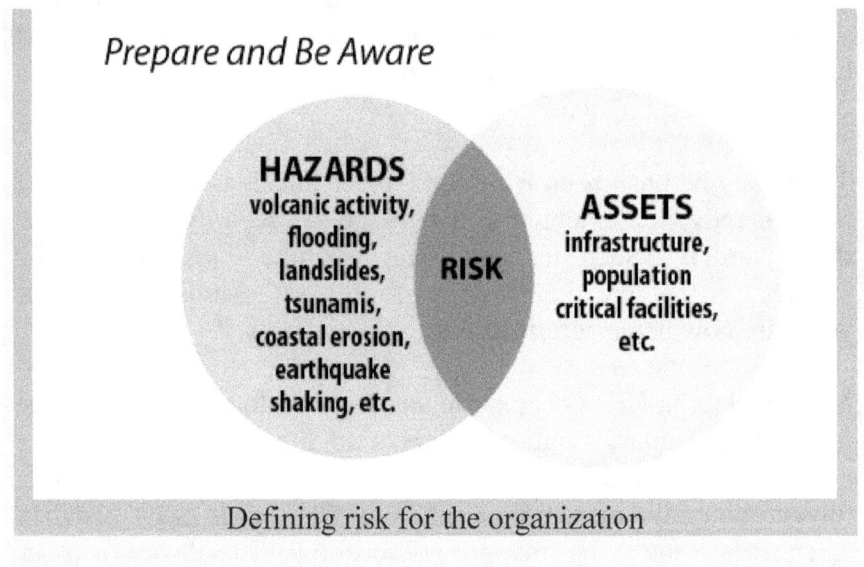

Prepare and Be Aware

HAZARDS
volcanic activity, flooding, landslides, tsunamis, coastal erosion, earthquake shaking, etc.

RISK

ASSETS
infrastructure, population critical facilities, etc.

Defining risk for the organization

50

http://www.hhs.gov/ocr/privacy/hipaa/administrative/securityrule/rafinalguidancepdf.pdf

DEMONSTRATION OF A RISK MANAGEMENT STRATEGY

The HIPAA practitioner will be well served by having a solid understanding of the risk management process. The better such a process is documented, the better the chances the organization will receive no major findings from a HHS OCR audit team.

Example of the threat and impact analysis process

The practitioner should develop an awareness of the need to create compliance documentation tracing the in-place technical controls to the perceived threat. This is a "reverse-engineering" approach to mapping technical safeguards to the threat/risk they addresses.

NOTE: Technical safeguards may include: firewalls, anti-virus software, e-mail SPAM filters, intrusion detection systems, open source vulnerability scanners, network traffic monitors, etc. "Soft" controls may include audit trails depicting authentication requests to Active Directory servers, log files of system access, network activity logs, etc.

ASSESSING IN-PLACE TECHNICAL CONTROLS

Fortunately for the practitioner many of these technical control categories are Addressable and may require unique documentation. This provides an opportunity to create documentation that (1) addresses the threat, and (2) address the HIPAA requirement. It is a way to leverage the HIPAA requirement to "kill two birds with one stone".

Having conducted a threat analysis brainstorming session with the I.T. technical staff, current technical controls can be mapped to identified threats. Then this mapping can be articulated in the form of an "Addressable" justification document for that control family and placed in the ARF.

For instance, in the I.T. technical enterprise area there are addressable control categories within the HIPAA Security Rule:

§ 164.308(a)(4)	Access Authorization
§ 164.308(a)(4)	Access Establishment and Modification
§ 164.308(a)(5)	Security Reminders
§ 164.308(a)(5)	Protection from Malicious Software
§ 164.308(a)(5)	Log-in Monitoring
§ 164.308(a)(5)	Password Management
§ 164.312(a)(1)	Automatic Logoff
§ 164.312(a)(1)	Encryption and Decryption
§164.312(c)(1)	Mechanism to Authenticate Electronic Protected Health Information
§ 164.312(e)(1)	Integrity Controls & Encryption

The reader will recall that Addressable does not mean optional, as noted by HHS OCR:

> ".. An addressable implementation specification is not optional; rather, if an organization determines that the implementation specification is not reasonable and appropriate, the organization must document why it is not reasonable and appropriate and adopt an equivalent measure if it is reasonable and appropriate to do so..."[51]

Therefore, if the technical controls are not specifically implemented, or if compensating controls shall be relied upon in their place, a memorandum is required to articulate this position. Such memorandums can be used to demonstrate mapping (traceability) to the original threat (and by default the HIPAA requirement).

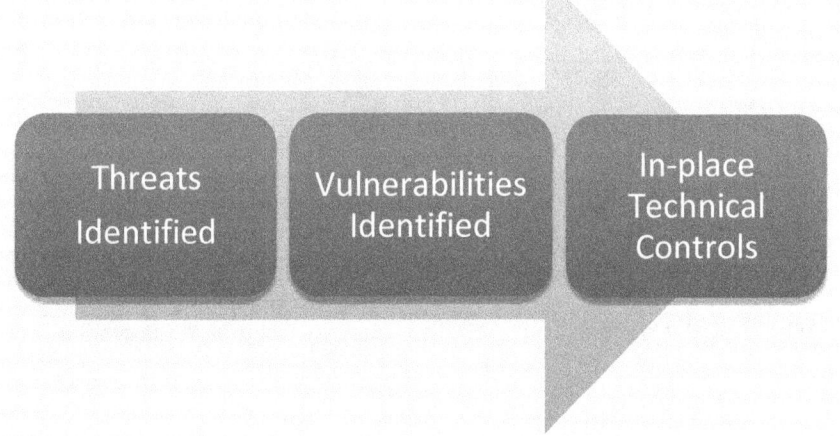

The traditional manner in which safeguards should be deployed.

---

[51]

http://www.hhs.gov/ocr/privacy/hipaa/administrative/securityrule/rafinalguidancepdf.pdf

In sum, the appropriate memorandums required for the Addressable requirements portion of the HIPAA Security Rule can also double as documents that map the safeguards to the identified risks. This demonstrates a risk management process.

Documenting the in-place safeguards with Addressable memorandums should reference the control family references in the NIST SP 800-53 (rev. 4) control categories to strengthen their authority. For instance, the NIST SP 800-53 (rev 4) control/safeguard categories are mapped to the HIPAA safeguard category in the following table:[52]

NIST SP 800-53 rev 4 CONTROL FAMILY[53]	HIPAA SECURITY RULE CATEGORY
AC-3 - ACCESS ENFORCEMENT	Access Authorization
AC-1 - ACCESS CONTROL POLICY AND PROCEDURES	Access Establishment and Modification
SI-5 - SECURITY ALERTS, ADVISORIES, AND DIRECTIVES	Security Reminders
SI-3 - MALICIOUS CODE PROTECTION	Protection from Malicious Software
AC-7 - UNSUCCESSFUL LOGON ATTEMPTS	Log-in Monitoring
AC-2 - ACCOUNT MANAGEMENT	Password Management
AC-12 - SESSION TERMINATION	Automatic Logoff
SC-13 - CRYPTOGRAPHIC PROTECTION	Encryption and Decryption
AC-2 - ACCOUNT MANAGEMENT	Mechanism to Authenticate Electronic Protected Health Information
AC-17 – REMOTE ACCESS	Integrity Controls & Encryption

---

[52] http://web.nvd.nist.gov/view/800-53/Rev4/family?familyName=Access Control

[53] Caveat: when the reader observers tables that cross reference two different standards this is referred to as a crosswalk. Crosswalks are used to cite additional guidance to help illustrate the true nature of the control.

These control (safeguard) families (categories) can also be viewed at the web-site for quick reference (see below).

No.	Control	Priority	Low	Moderate	High
AC-1	ACCESS CONTROL POLICY AND PROCEDURES	P1	AC-1	AC-1	AC-1
AC-2	ACCOUNT MANAGEMENT	P1	AC-2	AC-2 (1) (2) (3) (4)	AC-2 (1) (2) (3) (4) (5) (11) (12) (13)
AC-3	ACCESS ENFORCEMENT	P1	AC-3	AC-3	AC-3
AC-4	INFORMATION FLOW ENFORCEMENT	P1		AC-4	AC-4
AC-5	SEPARATION OF DUTIES	P1		AC-5	AC-5
AC-6	LEAST PRIVILEGE	P1		AC-6 (1) (2) (5) (9) (10)	AC-6 (1) (2) (3) (5) (9) (10)
AC-7	UNSUCCESSFUL LOGON ATTEMPTS	P2	AC-7	AC-7	AC-7
AC-8	SYSTEM USE NOTIFICATION	P1	AC-8	AC-8	AC-8
AC-9	PREVIOUS LOGON (ACCESS) NOTIFICATION	P0			
AC-10	CONCURRENT SESSION CONTROL	P3			AC-10
AC-11	SESSION LOCK	P3		AC-11 (1)	AC-11 (1)
AC-12	SESSION TERMINATION	P2		AC-12	AC-12
AC-13	SUPERVISION AND REVIEW - ACCESS CONTROL				
AC-14	PERMITTED ACTIONS WITHOUT IDENTIFICATION OR AUTHENTICATION	P3	AC-14	AC-14	AC-14

Web-site for NIST SP 800-53 (rev 4) Security Controls[54]

OBTAINING HIPAA DOCUMENTATION
OF EXISTING TECHNICAL SAFEGUARDS

As an example, in the case of automatic log-off (§ 164.312(a)(1)) the system administrator may need to provide a copy of the configuration settings used on a remote data access server or a Microsoft Windows workstation policy that enforces session termination after a predetermined time window of inactivity. Screen shots of the actual "session terminated" message may be appropriate as well.

---

[54] http://web.nvd.nist.gov/view/800-53/Rev4/family?familyName=ACCESS CONTROL

HIPAA Security Rule	Addressable Specification	NIST SP 800-53 Security Controls
164.312(a)(2)(iii)	Automatic Logoff (A): Implement electronic procedures that terminate an electronic session after a predetermined time of inactivity.	AC-11, AC-12

Threat	Risk	Safeguard
Unauthorized user hijacks session that has been left unattended	Unauthorized user obtains access to system and ePHI	Configured servers to force session termination after 15 minutes of inactivity.

This documentation (described above) now serves two purposes: (1) it has "addressed" the use of a compensating control ("technical safeguard"), and (2) it can be used to address the threat of improper session hijacking of an unattended desktop session (closing session after 15 minutes – session lock-out).

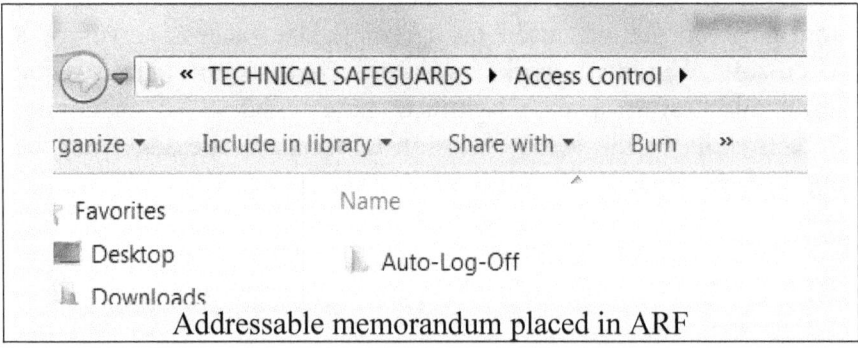

Addressable memorandum placed in ARF

SUMMARY

The subject of risk and risk management was again discussed. The risk perspective addressed in this chapter was centered around those technical controls that might be used to mitigate risk in an I.T. environment.

Dave Sweigert

XVI. CORRECTIVE ACTION PLANS

This chapter addresses the activity that is undertaken after a gap assessment has demonstrated the shortcomings of the institution's HIPAA compliance posture.

The purpose of a corrective action plan (CAP) is to map out a plan to implement a mitigation strategy to reduce the compliance gaps exhibited by the organization.

The CAP is the over-arching planning document that will be used to guide the execution of corrective actions to close the compliance gaps.

MITIGATION STRATEGIES

Correcting issues and addressing concerns is a method of mitigating risks. At this point, the organization has analyzed the threats and vulnerabilities that have reduced the HIPAA compliance posture of the institution.

As a foundational consideration all the gaps, vulnerabilities and threats should be reduced. This reduction is a form of mitigation. Mitigation is addressing these issues with corrective actions.

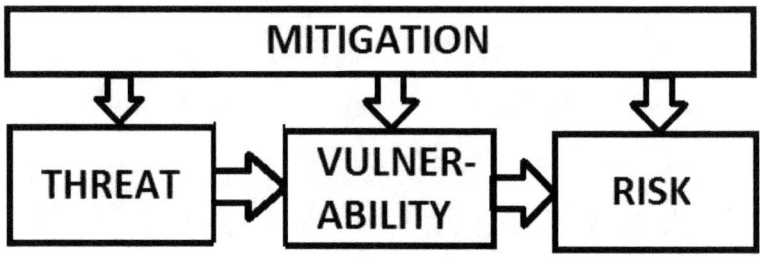

Example of the application of mitigation strategies

By this stage, risks have been prioritized by their level of severity. The risk of an unsecured back-door to the data center may be concerned a great threat than the lack of security awareness posters in the employee break room.

Once risks are known and prioritized, plans will need to address how these risks will be mitigated. In other words, what strategies will be employed to address the concern and reduce the impact a risk imposes upon the institution.

Threat	An active force that has the capability and desire to exploit a vulnerability. Taking advantage of a vulnerability.
Vulnerability	A weakness[55] or soft spot that can be exploited by a threat. A vulnerability per se does not mean it has been exploited.
Risk	A mathematical product that combines the probability that a vulnerability could be exploited to determine the overall risk to the organization.
Mitigation	Actions taken to reduce the level of risk to the organization. This may include obtaining insurance, increasing technical safeguards, etc.

Simply stated, a CAP is plan to manage the mitigation of the previously identified risks. The CAP process and documentation demonstrates to outsiders that the organization has indexed risks and has now developed plans to address such risks.

CHARACTERISTICS DRIVING CAPS

At the conclusion of a periodic risk assessment there may have been a dozen major vulnerabilities identified. Addressing the large number of risks/vulnerabilities may involve creating stand-alone documents that describe the vulnerability and provide a plan to address the concern.

---

[55] Timely mitigation of existing weaknesses, combined with the identification and mitigation of new weaknesses indicate that an operational POA&M process is in place. Prioritizations of such weaknesses reinforce the overall maturity of such a process. CENTERS FOR MEDICARE & MEDICAID SERVICES (CMS), POA&M GUIDELINES, July 2007

CORRECTIVE ACTION PLAN	
ISSUE 013	During threat assessment of 12/13/2014 it was discovered that the rear door of the facility could be easily pried open with a crow bar. The area is poorly lite and not alarmed.
Plan of Remediation	Prior to 3/3/15 there will be an external light mounted above the rear door of the complex. Prior to 4/4/15 the rear door will become alarmed with notification to a 24x7 alarm company.
Approval	Robert Overlooked Date

There are many conditions that may affect the timing of a corrective action. For instance, budgets may be tight and the corrective action cannot be purchased immediately. There may be other circumstances that impact corrective actions; such as a planned move, an upgrade to a computer system that was recently identified with vulnerabilities, etc.

Risks Identified	Remediation Planned	CAP Manages Remediation

The HHS OCR uses the same terminology – corrective action plan (CAP) – to resolve problems with institutions have been fined and sanctioned. Unfortunately, for these organizations, they have entered into a formal binding agreement with HHS OCR that has provisions for additional fines and sanctions if measurable progress is not made by the institution. Therefore, it is better to use a self-imposed CAP to correct problems (and demonstrate to HHS OCR the seriousness of the organization is addressing concerns).

PLAN OF ACTION & MILESTONES

A plan of action and milestones (POA&M) is an industry term that refers to a structured index that offers a detailed version of a CAP. The POA&M[56] is method to track the details of mitigations that address discrepancies and/or issues that have been identified in the CAP.

NOTE: Definition of a milestone. Milestones are the specific, action-oriented steps necessary to mitigate a weakness. The number of milestones articulated per weakness should directly correspond to the number of steps or corrective actions necessary to fully address and resolve the weakness. Each weakness must have at least one corresponding milestone with an anticipated completion date. The milestone completion date identifies the allotted time reserved to address the individual milestone and helps place milestones in a logical order.[57]

The goal is to document reasonable estimated date of completion (EDC) when corrective actions are expected to address the issue, concern or discrepancy. For example.

---

[56] A POA&M is a management process that outlines weaknesses and delineates the tasks necessary to mitigate them. CENTERS FOR MEDICARE & MEDICAID SERVICES (CMS), POA&M GUIDELINES, July 2007

[57] CENTERS FOR MEDICARE & MEDICAID SERVICES (CMS), POA&M GUIDELINES, July 2007

PLAN OF ACTION AND MILESTONES					
DISCRE-PANCY#	DESCRIP	CORREC. ACTION	START DATE	EST. DATE of COMP.	COMP. DATE
L-005	No malware detection device to identify worms, viruses, etc.	Deploy anti-virus software.	8/8/2015	9/9/2015	Pending
L-006	No shredders or other methods to dispose of paper PHI.	Procure a shredder vendor.	7/7/2015	9/9/2015	Completed on 8/16/15

REQUIRED RESOURCES TO CORRECT WEAKNESS

One of the objectives of the CAP & POA&M is to identify required resources needed to remediate the weakness. This can provide the business process owner with a tool to leverage resources to address such weaknesses. This can enable increased budgets and resources for the business owner or responsible coordinator.

NOTE. A mature POA&M process includes steps to validate the mitigation of weaknesses and ensures the accuracy of reported information. Estimated completion dates for weaknesses and milestones should be reviewed following the completion of a weakness. When the finding is a result of independent evaluation, the reviewer reviews the closed findings and determines if they have met the requirement, either by retesting or accepting the submitted documentation as proof of closure.[58]

SUMMARY

The use of Corrective Action Plans (CAPs) was addressed in this chapter. The use of a Plan of Action & Milestones (POA&M) was addressed as an appropriate tool to manage the CAP remediation process.

---

[58] CENTERS FOR MEDICARE & MEDICAID SERVICES (CMS), POA&M GUIDELINES, July 2007

EPILOGUE

Here ends Volume One. The reader should have achieved a working knowledge of the fundamental processes that need to be applied to the an enterprise to lay the foundation for an audit ready compliance program.

The author has chosen to stop at this point in order to devote a subsequent volume to the complexities of information security and assurance. Suffice to say, the knowledge contained in this present volume shall ensure the HIPAA novice is off to a good solid start in building a compliance program to support audit readiness.

END OF DOCUMENT

INDEX

ANNEX

ANNEX – A1
SAMPLE PRIVACY QUESTIONS

§164.520 , § 164.520(b)(1)
Is the Notice of Privacy Practices (NPP) posted in a prominent location visible to clients? If, applicable, where is the NPP posted?
Has the NPP been revised, amended or updated since the publication of the Final Omnibus Rule (see HIPAA Omnibus Rule for HITECH/ARRA, Jan. 17, 2013)?
Does the NPP match the description of the processes and procedures given to answer the questions above regarding accounting of disclosures, complaint resolution, access, denial of access or addition/amendments, etc.?

§ 164.530(a)
Who in your facility is designated as the primary point of contact to address concerns about HIPAA rules? Has this been specified in writing?
Is there a written policies that describes how you identified the staff members (employees or volunteers) or classes of persons who need access to PHI to carry out their duties that require training ?
Is there documentation that describes how the Privacy Official ensures that employees who handle PHI have access appropriate access to PHI needed to do their jobs
What policies and procedures describe any administrative methods used to ensure that only authorized workforce members receive access to e-PHI
Is there documentation that describes the periodic review cycle for policies and procedures
Is there documentation that describes the procedure for terminating access when a workforce member resigns, is terminated, suspended, retires or access is no longer needed?
If there is a change in law or rule (as with the HITECH – ARRA, OMNIBUS Rule) what documentation describes how policies and procedures are updated or revised to be in compliance with said new rules?

ANNEX – A2
SAMPLE PATIENT RIGHTS QUESTIONS

§ 164.524(a)
Do you have a formal process for individuals to access their health care records or request copies?
Have you developed procedures for the denial of access to PHI by individuals?
Do you have a formal process when a patient requests an amendment to his or her chart? What is your process if the patient requests to add an addendum to his or her chart?
Do you have a formal document that describes how you would deny accounting of disclosures?
Do you have a formal document that describes your procedures for using and disclosing PHI in relationship to health care treatment issues?
Under what circumstances are you involved with health care operations, such as performance of business functions for covered entities, licensing or certification, health care oversight, auditing or other functions that might involve contact with PHI?
If you collect PHI in the course of your business functions, what is your policy for subsequent disclosure of the PHI?
DESIGNATED RECORD SET: Do you have a Designated Record Set (DRS)?

ANNEX – A3
SAMPLE PHYSICAL SECURITY QUESTIONS

§164.310(a)(2)(ii)
Has your organization implemented written documentation that describes measures to provide physical protection for the ePHI in your possession?
Does your organization have documentation of your facility inventory, physical maintenance record, the history of physical changes, upgrades, and other modifications?
Does your organization have written procedures that address the physical security your facilities, including the exterior, the interior, and your equipment?
Does your organization have a facility security plan in place, under revision, or under development?
Has your organization developed a written security plan to protect the information system that contains ePHI?
Does your organization periodically review your facility security plan, is this in writing?
Does your organization update the facility security plan to address changes to the environment of operation or problems identified during plan implementation or security control assessments?
Does the facility have access card controlled doors? If YES, is there documentation that addresses this area -- or, describe the procedure to track access?
Are hard keys used by anyone in the facility? If YES, is there documentation that addresses this area or describes the procedure to manage the keys, including what happens if keys are lost or stolen?
Is there an alarm system in place during non-working hours? If YES, is there documentation that addresses this area or describes the procedures to inform users of alarm code changes and the frequency of the change process?

ANNEX – A4
SAMPLE SECURITY AWARENESS QUESTIONS

164.308(a)(5)(ii)(A)
Does your organization provide periodic security updates to your staff, employees, workforce, business associates and contractors or vendors?
Does your organization receive information system security alerts, advisories, and directives from designated external organizations on and on-going basis?
Does your organization disseminate security alerts, advisories, and directives to your defined list of individuals and offices?
What methods does your organization already have in place or use to keep your staff, employees, workforce, business associates and contractors or vendors updated and aware of security threats?
Does your organization provide security awareness training with all new hires before they are given access to ePHI?
Does your organization document and monitor individual information system security training activities including basic security awareness training and specific information system security training?
Does your organization have a process, a procedure, in place to ensure that everyone in your organization receives security awareness training

ANNEX – B

HHS RISK ASSESSMENT TOOL

In March of 2014 the HHS OCR, in cooperation with the Office of the National Coordinator for Health Information Technology (ONC), released a software tool that provides a guided walk-thru of a Security Risk Assessment (SRA)[59]. The SRA tool is limited to the HIPAA Security Rule (§§ 164.302 – 318) and may not be appropriate for assessing gaps in privacy policies, etc.

The SRA tool will help organizations meet the requirements for completing a risk assessment[60].

---

[59] http://www.hhs.gov/news/press/2014pres/03/20140328a.html
[60] Section 164.308(a)(1)(ii)(A). **RISK ANALYSIS (Required).** Conduct an accurate and thorough assessment of the potential risks and vulnerabilities to the confidentiality, integrity, and availability of electronic protected health information held by the [organization].

Security Risk Assessment

Integrating Privacy &
Security Into Your
Medical Practice

Health Information
Privacy and Security:
A 10 Step Plan

Health IT Privacy and
Security Resources

Mobile Device
Privacy and Security

Model Notices of
Privacy Practices

Patient Consent for
eHIE

Privacy & Security
Training Games

Cybersecurity

Security Risk Assessment Tool

What is the Security Risk Assessment Tool (SRA Tool)?

The Office of the National Coordinator for Health Information Technology (ONC) recognizes that conducting a risk assessment can be a challenging task. That's why ONC, in collaboration with the HHS Office for Civil Rights (OCR) and the HHS Office of the General Counsel (OGC), developed a downloadable SRA Tool [.exe - 66 MB] to help guide you through the process. This tool is not required by the HIPAA Security Rule, but is meant to assist providers and professionals as they perform a risk assessment.

We understand that users with Windows 8.1 Operating Systems may experience difficulties downloading the SRA Tool, we are working to resolve the issue and will post here when a resolution is identified and implemented.

http://www.healthit.gov/providers-professionals/security-risk-assessment-tool

ANNEX – C
SAMPLE POLICY FORMAT

FACILITY ACCESS CONTROLS	
TITLE:	VISITOR CONTROL POLICY
DATE:	MAR 3, 2015
NUMBER:	2005-A-004
APPROVED:	Mark Markenson, V.P. of Compliance
PURPOSE:	This policy has been defined to control the movement of contractors, third parties and other non-workforce members that access the controlled facility.
CITE:	164.310(a)(2)(iii) Standard: Facility access controls – Access control and validation procedures

ANNEX –D
NOTICE OF PRIVACY PRACTICES
CHECKLIST

Effective date. Ensure paper-based and electronic-based effective dates match.
Point of contact. Individual to receive all question and comments about the NPP.
Describe the facility that is following the notice. Street address, business address, etc. There may be ancillary sites that will not follow notice.
Pledge regarding medical information. Statements about commitment to securing patient data, safeguarding medical information.
Requirement to follow law. The NPP should address the need for the entity to follow the law to protect patient data.
Disclosure of medical information about the patient. A description of how and when the entity can disclose patient information. For example: disclosure by request of patient, for treatment, for payment, for health care operations, to designated family members, incidental disclosures, personnel involved in health care of patient, as required by law, to avert serious threat to health or safety, etc.
Right to inspect and correct. NPP should address the right of patient to update or modify medical information and/or request correction. Also known as Right to Amend.
Right to Accounting of Disclosures. NPP should address the ability of the patient to see who his/her medical information has been released to.
Right to Request Restrictions. NPP should address issues related to patient's request to limit exposure of medical information.
Changes to Notice. NPP should address how notification will be made to subscribers or patients concerning changes in the NPP.
Complaints. NPP should advise that a disgruntled patient or other party can contact the privacy official listed in the NPP, and, additional could contact the HHS OCR.

ANNEX – E
SAMPLE HIPAA AUDIT NOTIFICATION

DEPARTMENT OF HEALTH AND HUMAN SERVICES   OFFICE OF THE SECRETARY

Voice – (202) 619-0403 TDD – (202) 619-2357 FAX – (202) 619-3818
http://www.hhs.gov/ocr

Office for Civil Rights
200 Independence Ave., SW; RM 509F
Washington, DC 20201

Date
Name of Entity
Address of Entity
Point of Contact of Entity

Dear Covered Entity:

The Office for Civil Rights (OCR) of the Department of Health and Human Services (HHS) has responsibility for administration and enforcement of the Health Insurance Portability and Accountability Act (HIPAA) Privacy and Security Rules (45 CFR Part 160 and Part 164 Subparts C and E). These rules are designed to provide important health information privacy and security protections and rights for individuals. The OCR is committed to developing and enforcing strong health information privacy protections that do not impede access to quality health care.

The American Recovery and Reinvestment Act of 2009 (ARRA) requires HHS to audit covered entity and business associate compliance with the HIPAA privacy and security standards. To effectively implement this statutory mandate, OCR has engaged the services of a professional public accounting firm (KPMG LLP) to conduct performance audits, using generally accepted government auditing standards. You are receiving this letter because OCR has selected [Name of entity] to be the subject of an audit.

These audits are a new facet of the OCR health information privacy and security compliance program. Audits present an opportunity to examine mechanisms for compliance, identify best practices and discover risks and vulnerabilities that may not have come to light through OCR's established complaint investigations and compliance reviews. OCR will broadly share best practices gleaned through the audit process and guidance targeted to observed compliance challenges. OCR will assess whether to open a separate compliance review in cases where an audit indicates serious compliance issues.

Sample audit notification letter

174

ANNEX F
SAMPLE CORRECTIVE ACTION PLAN

Appendix A

CORRECTIVE ACTION PLAN BETWEEN

THE UNITED STATES DEPARTMENT OF HEALTH AND HUMAN SERVICES
AND
THE NEW YORK AND PRESBYTERIAN HOSPITAL

I.   Preamble

The New York and Presbyterian Hospital (NYP) hereby enters into this Corrective Action Plan (CAP) with the United States Department of Health and Human Services, Office for Civil Rights (HHS). Contemporaneously with this CAP, NYP is entering into a Resolution Agreement (Agreement) with HHS, and this CAP is incorporated by reference into the Resolution Agreement as Appendix A. NYP enters into this CAP as consideration for the release set forth in paragraph 8 of the Agreement.

II.   Contact Persons and Submissions

A.   Contact Persons.

NYP has identified the following individual as its contact person regarding the implementation of this CAP and for receipt and submission of notifications and reports:

> Aurelia G. Boyer, RN, MBA
> Senior Vice President & Chief Information Officer
> New York-Presbyterian Hospital
> aboyer@nyp.org

HHS has identified the following individual as its authorized representative and contact person with whom NYP is to report information regarding the implementation of this CAP:

> Linda C. Colon, Regional Manager, Region II
> Office for Civil Rights
> U.S. Department of Health and Human Services
> 26 Federal Plaza, Suite 3312
> New York, New York 10278
> Voice Phone (212) 264-4136
> Fax: (212) 264-3039
> Linda.Colon@HHS.gov

NYP and HHS agree to promptly notify each other of any changes in the contact persons or the other information provided above.

B.   Proof of Submissions.

Unless otherwise specified, all notifications and reports required by this CAP may be made by any means, including certified mail, overnight mail, or hand delivery, provided that

175

Dave Sweigert

ANNEX G
EXAMPLES OF NIST SP 800-53 (rev 4) PRIVACY CONTROLS

TABLE J-1: SUMMARY OF PRIVACY CONTROLS BY FAMILY

ID	PRIVACY CONTROLS
AP	**Authority and Purpose**
AP-1	Authority to Collect
AP-2	Purpose Specification
AR	**Accountability, Audit, and Risk Management**
AR-1	Governance and Privacy Program
AR-2	Privacy Impact and Risk Assessment
AR-3	Privacy Requirements for Contractors and Service Providers
AR-4	Privacy Monitoring and Auditing
AR-5	Privacy Awareness and Training
AR-6	Privacy Reporting
AR-7	Privacy-Enhanced System Design and Development
AR-8	Accounting of Disclosures
DI	**Data Quality and Integrity**
DI-1	Data Quality
DI-2	Data Integrity and Data Integrity Board
DM	**Data Minimization and Retention**
DM-1	Minimization of Personally Identifiable Information
DM-2	Data Retention and Disposal

Example of a NIST SP 800-53 (rev 4) Privacy Control

FAMILY: AUTHORITY AND PURPOSE

This family ensures that organizations: (i) identify the legal bases that authorize a particular personally identifiable information (PII) collection or activity that impacts privacy; and (ii) specify in their notices the purpose(s) for which PII is collected.

AP-1   AUTHORITY TO COLLECT

Control: The organization determines and documents the legal authority that permits the collection, use, maintenance, and sharing of personally identifiable information (PII), either generally or in support of a specific program or information system need.

Supplemental Guidance: Before collecting PII, the organization determines whether the contemplated collection of PII is legally authorized. Program officials consult with the Senior Agency Official for Privacy (SAOP)/Chief Privacy Officer (CPO) and legal counsel regarding the authority of any program or activity to collect PII. The authority to collect PII is documented in the System of Records Notice (SORN) and/or Privacy Impact Assessment (PIA) or other applicable documentation such as Privacy Act Statements or Computer Matching Agreements. Related controls: AR-2, DM-1, TR-1, TR-2.

Control Enhancements: None.

References: The Privacy Act of 1974, 5 U.S.C. § 552a (e); Section 208(c), E-Government Act of 2002 (P.L. 107-347); OMB Circular A-130, Appendix I.

Explanation of the control

Dave Sweigert

ABOUT THE AUTHOR

An Air Force veteran, Dave Sweigert began his immersion in the world of information security while assigned to the Electronic Security Command, San Antonia, Texas. Following active service, he worked as a defense contractor in the information security and networking fields for the U.S. Navy, U.S. Special Operations Command, U.S. National Security Agency, U.S. Army as well as the National Aeronautics and Space Administration. He has testified before the National Committee on Vital Heath Statistics as an expert concerning the progress of HIPAA implementation (2000). He is the former Statewide I.T. Security Policy Officer for the State of Ohio. He presently holds the following professional credentials: CISA, CISSP, HCISPP, PMP, Security+. He holds a Master's degree in Information Security from Capella University and a Master's degree in Project Management from Florida Institute of Technology. In his spare time he volunteers in community organizations as a licensed Emergency Medical Technician (B) and amateur radio operator. His late father, George H. Sweigert, is credited with the invention of the cordless telephone and was so issued a patent for same in 1969.

...

www.ingramcontent.com/pod-product-compliance
Lightning Source LLC
Chambersburg PA
CBHW051910170526
45168CB00001B/323